COSA

JEROME LECTURES

THIRTEENTH SERIES

COSA
THE MAKING OF A ROMAN TOWN

Frank E. Brown

ANN ARBOR

The University of Michigan Press

Library of Congress Cataloging in Publication Data
Brown, Frank Edward, 1908–
    Cosa, the making of a Roman town.

    (Jerome lectures ; 13th ser.)
    Includes bibliographical references.
    1. Ansedonia, Italy—Antiquities, Roman.
2. Excavations (Archaeology)—Italy—Ansedonia.
3. Romans—Italy—Ansedonia. 4. Italy—
Antiquities, Roman. I. Title. II. Series.
DG70.A587B76   937′.5   79–23668
ISBN 0–472–04100–2

298174

COSANIS UNIVERSIS DICATUS

Preface

In 1912 Thomas Spencer Jerome delivered at the American Academy in Rome a series of judicious lectures on the use of historical material. In one of these he remarked that "not only the affairs of the provinces but of Italy itself outside of Rome would be nearly blank to us, were it not for the evidence afforded by archaeology."[1] The ensuing sixty-six years have not failed to confirm Mr. Jerome's judgment, and it emboldens me to attempt in these chapters to sketch what I and my collaborators have learned from the excavation and study of its material remains about how a provincial Roman town took shape. The recorded history of Cosa, in fact, is confined to a notice of its founding and the report of a fresh addition to its citizens. This is scanty, if important, information. Cosa has revealed to us the rest of its history, step by step, since 1948 in fourteen short campaigns of excavation and many summers of joint study and interpretation.

Cosa, of course, could not have been unearthed and studied without the initiative of the American Academy in Rome, the collaboration of its fellows and the support of our many benefactors in the United States.[2] Our work could not have taken its course without the constant interest and generosity of the Marchesa Maria Rita San Felice Guglielmi, on whose land the ruins of Cosa repose. We must also acknowledge the cordial encouragement of the authorities of the Directorate General of Archaeology and Fine Arts and, above all, that of successive Superintendents of the Antiquities of Etruria: the late Antonio Minto, Giacomo Caputo, and Guglielmo Maetzke.

Notes

1. T. S. Jerome, *Aspects of the Study of Roman History* (New York, 1923), p. 424.

2. Columbia University, the State University of New York at Binghamton and Wesleyan University. The Bollingen and Old Dominion Foundations, the Samuel H. Kress Foundation and the National Endowment for the Humanities.

Contents

I: The Setting and the Promise

Cosa's history began before Cosa was born. During the summer of the year 280 B.C. the mobilized legions of Rome were deployed at the northern and southern extremities of her heterogeneous confederacy of city-states and tribes (fig. 1). One consular army faced the mercurial king of Epirus at Heraclea, on the instep of Italy and gave him his first, Pyrrhic victory. The other, commanded by the plebeian consul, Tiberius Coruncanius, met and crushed the combined levies of the Etruscan city-states of Volsinii and Vulci.[1]

Whether, during the preceding year, they had been in touch with Pyrrhus or whether it was merely the noise of his preparations that prompted them to join forces, Volsinii and Vulci made a last stand together against Rome's steady encroachment. Coruncanius had to march south hastily in defence of Latium and Rome against the king, but not before the terms of submission had been settled. Vulci and Volsinii were forced to join Rome's confederacy as unequal allies and, for their mistake, paid the customary indemnity of roughly one-third of their territory. The appropriated tracts were chosen with experienced foresight. They comprised Vulci's fertile coastal plain, adjoining that already confiscated from Tarquinia, and a broad strip of hilly country stretching inland from the coast to Volsinii's lake. The land was strategically situated and inviting to settlers. Its configuration would keep the restive cities apart and bar them from the sea. Its use and disposition for the good of the Commonwealth was evidently decided during the five years that elapsed before the final withdrawal of Pyrrhus from Italy. Two years later, in 273 B.C., the Latin colony of Cosa was planted, while the remainder was opened to Roman citizens for the equivalent of homesteading.[2]

In that year the Roman Republic stretched from the toe of Italy up the Tyrrhenian coast as far as Cosa and up the Adriatic to Sena Gallica, north of Ancona, with the still turbulent northwest frontier in between. It spread from sea to sea a patchwork of city-states and peoples standing in five distinct kinds and degrees of unifying relationship to Rome and to each other. At the top were the full Roman citizens, *optimo iure,* domiciled in the districts of the four urban and twenty-nine rustic tribes of the time, in six detached coastguard colonies and in scattered townships in Roman territory. Roman citizens of limited standing, *sine suffragio,* took second place. They were inhabitants of territories incorporated into the Commonwealth by conquest or voluntary submission, not Roman in speech or tradition. Although they performed such obligations of citizenship as paying direct taxes and serving in the army, they were not yet permitted to share in the conduct of Rome's affairs by voting or standing for office. On the other hand they kept a sort of double citizenship, continuing to participate in the affairs of their own towns. The third category comprised the ten Old Latin city-states, whose autonomy and institutions had been spared when Rome disbanded the Latin league in 338. The fourth was Rome's new Latin colonies, of which Cosa was the fifteenth since 338. The last and largest category consisted of Rome's allies, independent states that had submitted to be bound by treaty. It was their duty, specifically, to fight Rome's enemies, even if not their own, whenever summoned and, generally, *maiestatem populi Romani comiter conservare,* to preserve, as comrades, the sovereignty of the Roman people.

This manifold and dynamic structure of political entities had been devised empirically over the sixty-five years since Rome achieved her primacy in Latium. It had been built with unfailing resilience and common sense to further Rome's political aims and policies and to foster in her commonwealth an ever closer approximation to her institutions. Of its parts the Latin colonists, as the oldest and most tested, bore the brunt.

Rome, in effect, revived and continued the practice that had been followed by the Old Latin league, of which Rome had been first a member and then sole partner. The city-states of the league, from its unrecorded beginning down to the first quarter of the fourth century, had been accustomed, with the assent of their gods, to send out bands of their citizens to found new city-states for the purpose of defending and advancing the league's borders. These added Latin communities, once established, became full-fledged members of the league and enjoyed the fundamental privileges that bound the league together. Such were the rights of mutual and contractual trade, of lawful intermarriage, of exchange of domicile and citizenship from one city to another, of finding refuge in another city without losing one's original citizenship, and of regaining that citizenship when it had been lost involuntarily.[3]

This deliberate practice of integrated colonization had no precedent in the ancient world of its day. Greek colonization did not furnish a prototype. Even those *apoikiai,* settlements far from home, that may have been promoted or encouraged by states with imperialistic leanings, like Corinth or Miletos, remained proudly independent of their mother cities, acknowledging only formal religious, economic, or sentimental ties. In Italy the Sabines and Samnites, in both legendary and historical times, created new communities by their version of the widespread, primitive custom of fission in years of dearth. The *ver sacrum,* as it was called, consecrated, in the spring, the male offspring of that year to a god, normally Mars. Under his guidance, on reaching manhood, they were driven out to fend for themselves. At least one legend of Etruscan colonization—that of the founding of Capena from Veii—implies a *ver sacrum,* but the other scanty and fragmented legends of the Etruscan colonies planted in the Po Valley and in Campania are patently modeled on the Greek.[4]

The first of Rome's Latin colonies, Cales, planted in 334 B.C. on the northern border of Campania, established a new and fictitious Latin citizenship. It was related to Rome as the city-states of the Old Latin league, including Rome, had been related to one another, and was to have a long and purposeful life. The new Latin colonists were drawn from the existing Old Latin states, from Rome, and, as time went on, from the towns of Rome's second class citizens and from her allies. By volunteering to become Latin colonists they shed their original citizenship to assume the citizenship of their colony. In so doing, they acquired, with respect to Rome and their sister colonies, all the same reciprocal rights that the cities of the Old Latin league had enjoyed, including the obligation to serve in Rome's armies, as required, for sixteen out of thirty years up to age forty-six.[5]

Having been conceived in the image of an Old Latin colony, the new Latin colony was otherwise an independent, self-governing city-state, endowed with a surrounding territory of a size to support it. Like any independent state, it elected its own magistrates to conduct its public business according to its own laws, administering justice in its own courts. It levied its own taxes, maintained its own troops, and financed its own public works. The outward signs of its autonomy were the coins of bronze and silver it had power to strike and its appointed ambassadors, who treated of its exceptional affairs with Rome and other city-states in Italy.[6]

The ability of a given Latin colony to grow and develop would depend on the natural resources of its territory and the industry of its colonists. Our words "colonist" and "colony" were Latin *colonus* and *colonia,* derived from the verb *colo, colere* "to farm." A *colonus* was a farmer and a *colonia* a settlement of farmers. In the special sense of colonist and colony these terms had not lost their generic meaning. A colonist was first of all a farmer. Each Latin colonist was from the outset allotted a parcel of land to farm and presumably the right to graze his livestock and fell timber on the public domain. From the Roman point of view this was essential, not only to the economy of the colony but also to the good of the Commonwealth.[7]

Rome's dominion was founded on manpower, but not all its manpower was available for military service. Only those citizens who had a sufficient stake in the Commonwealth were acceptable. The soundest stake was land and the best soldier a farmer. In those days the Roman soldier was required to outfit himself with his own armor and weapons at his own expense. Citizens who could not afford to equip themselves were of no use as military manpower. It was especially these poorer citizens who were attracted by the prospect of enrolling themselves in a colony. Their acquisition of land gave them their stake and made them soldiers, soldiers of their colony, but soldiers also available to Rome. Of course, from the colonist's point of view, this was not always the most enticing prospect. Like most colonists in all times and places, including our forefathers, the source of attraction was the fresh start, with a grubstake, in changed surroundings, and the chance of a new identity, a new and better life.[8]

The new Latin colonies, again, carried on, in a more rapidly expanding Commonwealth, the function that the colonies of the Old Latin league had performed. They were established at critical points on Rome's advancing frontiers, bordering on newly subjugated and undependable allies, facing the hostile neighborhood beyond. They were the outposts of the Republic, *speculae populi Romani* and *propugnacula imperii,* as Cicero liked to call them long after. As such they were strongly fortified and manned for the defence of what had been won, ready to become bases for future offensives. Their initial role in Roman strategy was therefore military, but, as fixed and lasting city-states in pacified surroundings, they were inevitably destined to become vital centers for the dissemination of Roman attitudes, institutions, law and language.[9]

During the sixty-one years between the founding of Cales in 334 B.C. and Cosa in 273, fifteen Latin colonies are known to have been established. This works out to a rate of one colony every four years, although they were not founded with such regularity. In each of three of these groups of years pairs of foundings are recorded; in another a triplet. In any case, given the time required to make the decision, choose the site, plan the town, survey the territory, enroll the colonists and provide them with the bare essentials for making a start, it will be evident that a virtually continuous activity of colonial preparation and realization, performed by a numerous, professional staff, was being carried on in Rome and on site year after year.[10]

Our sources of information reveal only the managers of this activity. The Roman senate made the decision. The enabling act, which specified the location of the colony, the number of colonists, the composition of the supervisory board of Commissioners and probably the funds at its disposal, was voted by the Plebeian Assembly. The Commissioners, normally three of the more eminent senators, were elected in the Tribal Assembly. Their term of office was usually fixed at three, but some times more, years, since they were in full charge of the procedure of founding the colony and administering its staff. Although the sole meager and tendentious source that records this infrastructure is not contemporary, the tasks of any colonial commission would of necessity be very much the same and the personnel would inevitably include surveyors, engineers, and architects, clerks, accountants, and archivists.[11]

The territory selected for the Latin colony of Cosa was the northwestern part of the lands that had been taken from Vulci by Coruncanius in 280 (fig. 2). It comprised an ample mainland tract, stretching as far as 12½ miles (20 km.) inland from the coast, and a seaboard tract composed of the coastal lagoons of Vulci on the south and of Orbetello to the west, with the long sand bars and the island promontory of Mount Argentario that enclosed it (fig. 3). Two offshore islands, Igilium (Giglio) and Dianium (Gianutri), named for its crescent shape, guarded the sea approaches.

The sum total of land and lagoon was some 213 square miles (about 550 square km.). The territory was bounded on the north by the Albegna river, its tributaries, the Elsa and Elsarella, and the watershed of the mountain mass above their source. On the east, the boundary descended to the coast along the Tafone stream, only four miles (6 km.) from the walls of Vulci.[12]

The coastal lowlands (fig. 4) and the river plain of the Albegna, together with the broad valleys that reached inland from both, would make the best farmland. Their deep, ferruginous earth was overlaid with alluvial and lagoon deposits and watered perennially by streams. The uplands, rising gently above them, would provide good grazing and well-exposed slopes for the vine and the olive. Higher still the hillsides were covered with fir and pine, oaks, beech, maple, and sycamore, ready for the axe. The maritime aspects of the territory held other resources. The shallow lagoons (figs. 5 and 6), fed by the streams from the hinterland, would be natural landlocked fisheries as well as waterways for local transportation. The coastal waters and the channel between the islands and Mount Argentario abounded in all sorts of smaller fish from mackerel to sardines, while early each summer there were great runs of tunny.[13]

A narrow strip of land between a rough mountain mass and the lagoon of Orbetello makes a corridor for travel between the coastal lowland and the valley of the Albinia. All the traffic on land up and down the coast must pass through it, even today. At its southern end rises the hill (fig. 7), known since the Middle Ages as Ansedonia, jutting for half its circumference into the sea above the two lagoons and opposite Mount Argentario. This was the site that had been chosen for the town of Cosa. It was not only a site of rare beauty but also a vantage point as well.

The hill (fig. 8) is a mass of light gray, dolomitic limestone, riddled with natural fissures and caverns. Roughly oval in shape, it rises above the water some 375 feet (114.00 m.). Along the seaward arc sheer cliffs drop 65 to 145 feet (20.00–45.00 m.), interrupted only on the southwest by a tiny cove. The ascents above are steep and craggy, save on the north and northeast, where a ridge and gentler slopes are more easily negotiable. To a Roman's eye it looked high and rugged enough to be easily defensible, but not too high and rugged to be readily accessible. Beside its eastern foot, moreover, the broad valley rising from the coastal plain to merge northward over a low pass with another descending to the Albegna, would provide a direct route to the territory taken from the Volsinians. It was an excellent position, in the tradition of Roman hill towns and inland colonies, to check Vulci and Volsinii, to support the Roman settlers moving into the confiscated lands on the north and east, and to block the Etruscans further north.

The choice of a strong position by the sea promised further advantages. In the years following the struggle with Pyrrhus the Roman senate was preoccupied by sea power and the looming confrontation with Carthage. The promontory of Argentario and the island of Giglio were obligatory points of call for all naval and mercantile vessels moving between Rome and Corsica, Sardinia, Gaul, or Spain over the coastal passage by way of Planasia and Elba. Between the hill of Ansedonia and Mount Argentario there stretched a broad bay shielded from the westerly and northerly winds (fig. 3). Facing it, the indented, eastern coast of Argentario presented a capacious, sheltered cove between high hills, ancient and modern Porto Ercole, perhaps already in use as a harbor. The eastern cliffs of Ansedonia, ending in a jutting point (fig. 7), fell steeply to the long lagoon of Vulci and screened an anchorage by the dunes. Close at hand were the timber and naval stores needed to create the fleets Rome might soon be building. It may be recalled that Cosa's twin Latin colony of the year 273 was Paestum, 250 miles (400 km.) away on the coast of Lucania. Both colonies reflected the same naval strategy, the same anticipation of events. But commerce would follow the flag, and what might serve for war would serve for peace. The colony was situated to prosper, eventually, by trade.[14]

The Romans found the hill of Ansedonia uninhabited. Our excavations, indeed, have yielded nothing to suggest that it had ever been inhabited. At the same time the colonial territory appears to have been very sparsely settled. Not so in earlier times. From the seventh century B.C. on into the fifth the highlands behind the coastal plain from Marsigliana on the north around to Pescia Romana on the east, were dotted with larger or smaller Etruscan settlements, whose existence is attested now only by their cemeteries. During the two centuries before 273 they had dwindled and disappeared, leaving an as yet inexplicable blank. There was, however, one exception, the Etruscan town at the tip of the peninsula in the midst of the lagoon of Orbetello (fig. 5). Its cemeteries stretched from the outskirts of medieval and modern Orbetello to the base of the peninsula. From 1820 onward their grave goods were looted and dispersed by the landowners under whose properties they lay. Fortunately enough has survived in collections and in the reports of contemporary witnesses to demonstrate that the cemeteries had been in use without a break from the seventh to at least the first century B.C. This, then, must have been the town, originally called Cusi* or Cusia* in Etruscan, that gave its name to Latin Cosa on the hill. In time to come it would continue to thrive alongside New Cosa on its fisheries and its local traffic across the lagoon.[15]

Before this territory and town site would be ready to receive its occupants there was much for the triumvirate of commissioners and their staffs of technicians to do. The territory had to be accurately delimited and mapped. The boundaries of the town with its access roads and gates, its street plan with its public and private zones, the positions of its essential public spaces and its individual house plots had to be determined, defined, and staked out. The colonists had to be assured an adequate water supply and the provisions to sustain them until their first crop was harvested. All this, in the year or years preceding the arrival of the colonists, would have been planned and carried out following a routine derived from recurrent practice and modified empirically according to circumstances.

The surveyors were first required to establish a uniform grid of squares or rectangles, applicable to the entire territory, for the purpose of marking the boundaries of the public domain with respect to the lands to be assigned to the individual colonists. It was then their duty to divide these farmlands, according to the number of freeholders, into plots of a given area, separated at intervals by roads or tracks and then to designate the plots according to the coordinates of the grid, setting up permanent markers, and entering them in a register of freeholds. The surveyors worked with the simple but serviceable instruments that all surveyors used up to the invention of the telescope: the surveyor's staff and cross for sighting and the surveyor's chain or cord for measuring. Their task was not lightened by the physical features of the territory. The good farmland, of which there was plenty and to spare, lay in tracts separated by intervening ridges and mountains.[16]

The overall Cosa grid appears to have been based on the right angle formed by the Albegna and the coastal strip along the lagoon of Old Cosa (fig. 2). A surveyor stationed on the hill of Cosa could at one sighting establish a base line through the corridor between the mountains and the lagoon on across the Albegna valley and another base line at right angles across the coastal lowland and the open valley opposite, thus linking the two major compartments of farmland. The second base line has been identified and indicates that the surveyor had set up his cross or *groma* on the boundary of the town site where its northeast gate would stand. Other elements of the grid in the shape of roads and field walls have been located in both compartments with the help of maps and air photographs. These confirm the orientation of the grid, 56 degrees east of north, and the distance of its intervals, 638 yards (568.00 m.) or sixteen *actus,* the Roman surveyor's unit. No traces that might furnish a clue to the exact size of the original allotments have yet come to light. They would hardly have been larger, though, than about five acres (2 hect.). [17]

The planning of the town to be laid out on the top of Cosa's hill joined surveyors to engineers and architects (figs. 8 and 9). The hilltop itself was flattish and tilted up toward the south where twin summits were joined by a broad, nearly level saddle. The slope, the saddle, and the heights would be the physical determinants of the plan. The wall which would bound the town was traced to enclose these features and to follow the natural contours of the hillside just below the verge. Within its perimeter of about $9/10$ mile (1.5 km.) it enclosed some 32 ⅔ acres (13.25 hect.). The gaps in it for gates were placed at the lowest points on the northwest, northeast, and southeast fronts, where the access roads from below entered. The one that mounted the northwest ridge was the road from Portus Herculis across the sandbar. Halfway up the northeastern slopes two roads joined and climbed to the gate. One was the road from Marsigliana on the Albegna, through the valleys and across the coastal plain. The other led up from the end of the lagoon of Vulci and the anchorage in the lee of the hill, whence the road up the steeper, southeast slope also came. An opening was left, too, for a postern gate in the southwest front, where a track from the little cove below passed through.

The southern summit at the apex of the town site, though it lifted only a few yards above the eastern height, dominated the site, the sweep of the territory within view and the seascape. Low cliffs along its northwest flank isolated it from the gentle slope beneath. It formed the natural high place to be made sacred, the acropolis or Arx of Cosa, and its rocky crest was planed down to make a level platform (fig. 10). The saddle to the northeast afforded the only ample and approximately level area on the site. Although off-center, its proximity to the adjacent gates and roads that led down to the lagoon and anchorage made it the obvious location for the civic center, the Forum, with its eventual public spaces. Here, for a beginning, a long, rectangular gathering place was laid out within a larger area bounded by streets.

The given position of the Arx, the Forum and the gates, together with the pitch of the terrain, governed the street plan. This, too, like the survey of the territory, but unrelated to it, was an orthogonal grid. Its orientation seems to have been motivated without regard to celestial imperatives but rather by two mundane concerns. The streets were to have the most moderate and uniform grade possible as they crossed the slopes, to be terraced in the future, and they should bring the Forum into axial and visual relation with the Arx and the northwest gate. The result was a satisfactory compromise, yielding a functional but not uniform network which ran diagonal to the cardinal points, 39 and 51 degrees from true north.

The three streets leading to and from the gates constituted the arterial system of the plan. None ran straight through from gate to gate. All crossed and merged in the center of the town, skirting and penetrating the area of the Forum. They were meant to channel all the traffic from within or without through the town by way of the center or to and from the center and the periphery. These thoroughfares and their tributary streets divided the site into rectangular blocks of unequal size and somewhat irregular in shape where they bordered the pomerial road along the boundary. It is likely that not quite all the streets that were laid out have been recognized, but all that have been, with three exceptions, were evidently plotted out at a uniform width of twenty feet. The exceptions were the entryways at either end of the Forum square and the two processional streets that linked the Arx and the Forum and connected the Forum and the eastern height. These were given a width of thirty feet.[18]

In conjunction with the plotting of the town plan and the boundary, four large tanks were hewn out of the rock in order to collect a reserve of water for the colonists. The hill of Cosa, like the other limestone hills and mountains round about, was waterless. Rainfall either ran off or percolated through the porous texture of the rock to emerge at the foot in perennial alkaline springs. These, though not sweet, would do for the day-by-day drinking, cooking, and washing, but in case of emergency, siege, or blockade rainwater was indispensable. The tanks were carefully situated, two half way down and two at the bottom of the site, so as to capture and collect the runoff from the slopes above. Squarish and some 11½ feet (3.50 m.) deep, walled with large polygonal blocks where the rock gave out and lined with watertight cement, they could hold about 790,000 gallons (3,000,000 l.). They would be filled during the autumn and winter before the colonists reached their new home.

At this point it may be worth comparing the work of Cosa's surveyors with that of two earlier Latin colonies, Norba and Alba Fucens. Planted on similar hilltop sites and preserving many of their original features, both have been explored and partially excavated. Norba had been an Old Latin colony, which, in 342, was sacked by its Volscian neighbors. A few years later the site was repopulated and at the same time planned and fortified. The new town represents the stage of Roman ideas and practice in planning sites like these at the beginning of its Latin colonization (fig. 11).[19]

The wall that girdled Norba's spectacular position, 1,640 feet (500.00 m.) above the Pontine marshes, enclosed a flattened hilltop, much like Cosa's, falling southwestward from two crests toward the east, which were joined by a broad saddle. The crests became the sacred high-places. A somewhat irregular grid of streets and terraces was flexibly applied to the less precipitous slopes, following the natural lay of the land. This orientation, rather than unifying the town site, tended to separate it into upper and lower units. The major axis ran from a postern gate across the lower town to the lesser high-place. Here it would have been linked by a right-angle jog to the main gate at the eastern extremity of the site. A street from the secondary north gate appears to have swung south eastward toward the wide, level terraces below the major high-place. This may well have been the area of the Forum, reachable also from the main gate.

Alba of the Fucine lake was founded a generation later, midway in time between Norba and Cosa (fig. 12). Its elongated hilltop was cupped by three heights, north, east, and south, and by a long western ridge. The northern and higher summit, undoubtedly its original high-place, lies buried under the ruins of the medieval village of Albe. The other two were crowned by temples, independent of the grid of streets that was confined to the central depression. Arterial thoroughfares to and from the west, northwest, and southeast gates determined the location of the Forum and the rectangular blocks of unequal size around it. They functioned as radiants, less completely articulated than at Cosa, and carried the highway, Via Valeria, from Rome to the Adriatic through the town.[20]

These three Latin colonies, in similar topographical situations, manifest a progression in planning from the crude and disjointed effort at Norba, through the incompletely realized, radial network at Alba, to the neatly unified solution at Cosa. Each was a study in orthogonal planning, a premeditated design for what a functioning Roman environment ought to be. The unplanned, radial prototype was Rome itself. These rectilinear versions, based on the past and intended for the future, expressed their lineage, their likeness and their progress.

Notes

1. Fasti Triumphales Capitolini, *Inscriptiones Italiae* 13, pp. 1, 73, 545; Appian, *Sam.* 10. 3; Zonaras, 8. 4; Livy, *Per.* 11. Cf. K. J. Beloch, *Römische Geschichte* (Weimar, 1925), p. 455; A. Afzelius, *Die römische Eroberung Italiens* ("Acta Jutlandica," aarschrift for AArhus Universitet, 14, 3, Copenhagen, 1942), pp. 69, 117, 189; P. Lévèque, "Pyrrhos," *BEFAR* 185 (1957): 337–39; A. J. Toynbee, *Hannibal's Legacy,* vol. 1 (London, 1965), p. 150.

2. Velleius, 1. 14. 7; Livy, *Per.* 14; Pliny, *NH* 3. 51. Viritane allotments: *praefectura* Saturnia, Festus, 262 L, cf. Livy, 39. 55. 9; *praefectura* Statonia, Vitruvius, 2. 7. 3, Pliny, *NH* 36. 168. Beloch, *Römische Geschichte,* p. 455; Afzelius, *Die römische Eroberung Italiens,* p. 183 f.; Toynbee, *Hannibal's Legacy,* pp. 178, 239; E. T. Salmon, *Roman Colonization under the Republic* (London, 1969), p. 189, n. 202.

3. M. Gelzer, "Latium," *RE* 12, no. 1 (1924): 940–63; Salmon, *Roman Colonization under the Republic,* pp. 40–54; A. N. Sherwin-White, *Roman Citizenship*[2] (Oxford, 1973), pp. 7–37, 96–118; A. Bernardi, *Nomen Latinum* ("Studia Ghisleriana," Pavia, 1973), pp. 9–76.

4. W. Eisenhut, "Ver Sacrum," *RE* 8A, no. 1 (1955): 911–23; J. Heurgon, *Trois Etudes sur la "Ver Sacrum"* ("Collection Latomus," 26, 1957).

5. Cales: Livy, 8. 16. 14; Velleius, 1. 14. 3. Military service: Polybius, 6. 19. 2; Cicero, *De Senectute* 17. 60; Livy, 43. 14. 6; Gellius, *NA* 10. 28. Cf. G. De Sanctis, *Storia dei Romani,* vol. 2 (Florence, 1953), p. 197; Toynbee, *Hannibal's Legacy,* pp. 424–37.

6. Toynbee, *Hannibal's Legacy,* pp. 249–58; Salmon, *Roman Colonization under the Republic,* pp. 85–87.

7. Cato, *Agr.* preface 2; Festus, 35L. Cf. A. Rudorff, *Die Schriften der römischen Feldmesser,* vol. 2 (Berlin, 1852), pp. 395–99; O. A. W. Dilke, *The Roman Land Surveyors* (Newton Abbot, 1971), pp. 107, 113, 124, 172.

8. Cato, *Agr.* preface 4. Polybius, 6. 22–23; Livy, 8. 8.; cf. Toynbee, *Hannibal's Legacy,* pp. 505–18.

9. Cicero, *pro Font.* 13. P. Fraccaro, "L'organizzazione politica dell'Italia romana," *Atti del Congresso Internazionale di Diritto Romano* 1 (1933): 195–208.

10. E. Kornemann, "Coloniae," *RE* 4 (1901): 515; Salmon, *Roman Colonization under the Republic,* pp. 55–63. Cf. W. V. Harris, *Rome in Etruria and Umbria* (London, 1971), p. 158 f.

11. E. Kornemann, "Coloniae," *RE* 4 (1901): 568–71; Salmon, *Roman Colonization under the Republic,* p. 19, Cicero, *Leg. Agr.* 2.32

12. R. Cardarelli, "Confini fra Magliano e Masiliana; fra Manciano e Montauto Scerpenna Stachilagi; fra Tricosto e Ansedonia; fra Orbetello e Marsiliana; fra Port'Ercole e Monte Argentario (28 dicembre 1508–2 marzo 1510)," *Maremma, Bollettino della Società Storica Maremmana* 1 (1924): 182–86, 206–21; G. Merciai,

"Sulle condizioni fisiche del litorale etrusco fra Livorno e Civitavecchia," *StEtr* 3 (1929): 355 f.

13. Soils: L. H. Davis, *Roman Population Distribution in the Ager Cosanus,* B.A. Thesis, Wesleyan University, Middletown, 1976, pp. 73–120. Timber: G. Santi, *Viaggio secondo per le due provincie senesi* (Pisa, 1798), pp. 97–203. Fishery: Strabo, 5. 2. 8.; R. Del Rosso, *Pesche e peschiere antiche e moderne* (Florence, 1905), vol. 1, pp. 70–97; vol. 2, pp. 310–451; P. Raveggi, *Orbetello Antica e Moderna* (Grosseto, 1933), p. 52 f.

14. F. E. Brown, "Cosa I: History and Topography," *MAAR* 20 (1951): 12 f.

15. A. Minto, Marsiliana d'Albegna (Florence, 1921); D. Levi, "Escursione archeologica nell'agro cosano," *StEtr* 1 (1927): 477–85; S. L. Dyson, "Settlement Patterns in the Ager Cosanus," *NSc* (forthcoming): 10–12. Necropolis of Orbetello: *Nuova collezione di opuscoli,* vol. 1 (Florence, 1820), p. 131; F. Carchidio, *Memorie storiche dell'antico e moderno Telamone,* vol. 1 (Florence, 1824), pp. 75–109; G. B. Thaon, "Scavi fatti nell vicinanze di Orbetello," *Antologia* 33 (1829): 138–40; *BdI* (1829): 7f.; *BdI* (1830): 254; *BdI* (1849): 66–68; *BdI* (1851): 7–9, 37 f., 147–49; *BdI* (1858): 103–5; *BdI* (1867): 145–47; *NSc* (1927): 210–13; *NSc* (1936): 408–13. Objects recovered in Vatican Museum; G. Micali, *Monumenti inediti,* 328 = *Musei Etruschi* (1842): 1, tab. 10 = Helbig, *Führer*[4] I (1963): 521, no. 691; in Archaeological Museum of Florence; *NSc* (1885): 241–48; in Antiquarium of Orbetello; M. Santangelo, *L'antiquarium di Orbetello* (Rome, 1954), pp. 9–33. Etruscan name of Orbetello: M. Pallottino, "Nomi etruschi di città," *Scritti in onore B. Nogara* (Rome, 1937), pp. 343–45, 352, 354, 356.

16. *Limitatio* and *groma:* Rudorff, *Die Schriften der römischen Feldmesser,* pp. 335–37; Salmon, *Roman Colonization under the Republic,* pp. 20–24; Dilke, *The Roman Land Surveyors,* pp. 27, 66–70, 73.

17. F. Castagnoli, "La centuriazione di Cosa," *MAAR* 24 (1956): 149–65; *Le ricerche sui resti della centurazione* (Rome, 1958), pp. 15, 24, 26, 27; F. T. Hinrichs, *Die Geschichte der gromatischen Institutionen* (Wiesbaden, 1974), pp. 29 f., 48, 82.

18. Brown, "Cosa I: History and Topography," *MAAR* 20 (1951): 23–27.

19. Livy, 7. 42. 8; 8. 1. 1–4; *NSc* (1901): 514–59; *NSc* (1903): 229–62; *NSc* (1904): 403–30; G. Schmiedt and F. Castagnoli, "L'antica città di Norba," *L'universo* 37 (1957): 125–48.

20. Livy, 10. 1. 1; J. Mertens, "Etude topographique d'Alba Fucens," *Alba Fucens,* vol. 1 (Brussels, 1969), pp. 37–118.

II: The Founding and the Lean Years

The territory and the town site of the Latin colony of Cosa had been readied by the practiced staff, headed by the colonial Commissioners. It now awaited its colonists, assembled in Rome. What of them?

One can only venture a more or less informed guess. It is likely that, at this time, most would have been full Roman citizens, some from the Old Latin states and others, perhaps, from the second-class Roman towns, hence Italians. With one exception, all the names to be culled from the sparse inscriptions found at Cosa are Latin, if not Roman. For the most part the colonists would have been of the poorer sort. We can assume that the greater number were unsuccessful or unsatisfied farmers, but that a good many were craftsmen, tradesmen, and, probably, seamen and fishermen. They were a chance, heterogeneous group, with no ties beyond their common urge to move on and their fundamental equality as citizens of a new city-state. Whatever their origins, they had known no other social or political order than that of the aristocratic city-state. In their new community they would be expected, as a matter of course, to fall into place in the old, inherent order at the disposition of the Commissioners. First of all, at the start of the journey toward the promised land, the Commissioners would have marshaled them in their new military units, their cohorts, and appointed the prefects to lead them.[1]

How many were they? The erratic record of the numbers of Latin colonists refers in each case, not to whole populations but to male heads of families, that is to say available military manpower. Cosa's figure is not recorded, but by 273 three standard sizes of colony were current. The smallest, of 2,500 families, is last heard of in 314, but the figures for half the colonies down to Cosa are missing. The next largest size, of 4,000 families, appears in 313 and the largest, of 6,000 families, in 303 at Alba Fucens. The relatively limited area within the perimeter of Cosa clearly suggests that it was a small colony. In fact, the actual size of its area when compared with the area enclosed by the original walls of Alba Fucens reflects the ratio of 2,500 to 6,000 family units. More significantly this was also the ratio of the sizes of their forum squares, which had been laid out to accommodate the public activities of all the citizens of either colony. By implication the figure of 2,500 families represents something like 9,000 free men, women, and children.[2]

One may imagine them setting out from Rome on a mid-summer morning in 273: the Commissioners and their retinue on horseback, riding ahead or patrolling the flanks of the column; the able-bodied men and boys learning to march under the banners of their cohorts; the rest walking or riding on their ox carts, piled high with goods and gear, with the other livestock hitched behind. The motley column must have strung out for at least sixteen miles (25 km.). Cosa lay only seventy miles (113 km.) away as the crow flies, but it was ninety miles (145 km.) by the ancient Via Aurelia, and that paved trunk road did not yet exist. Our column would have followed country lanes and tracks, linking the Etruscan cities along the way. At the pace of an ox cart on dirt roads, a long day's journey might cover, at best, sixteen miles. Perhaps on the morning of the sixth day the vanguard sighted the hill ahead and reached it in the afternoon. The end of the column came up a day later.

Once they were assembled again and encamped on the town site, Cosa could assume its name and be established. In that world, of which the city-state was the basic unit and in which every important political act was divinely sanctioned, the birth of a new city-state was the most momentous. Only the will of the gods could create it and they must first be summoned. In this case Jupiter Latiaris, Jupiter of the Latins, would have been invoked.

In front of the leveled platform of rock, on the highest peak of the hill and a little below it, a natural cleft in the rock had been shaped into a deep, squarish pit (fig. 13). There, before dawn, the augur, accompanied by one of the Commissioners, took his stand, facing the highest mountain peak on the horizon a little east of north over the pit. On this line of sight his field of vision, coincident with the surveyor's grid of the land, encompassed the town site and its territory. He traced his sacred square on the platform, projected it on the landscape and the tract of sky above, calling upon the god and naming the signs that would declare his presence and approval. Then, as the sun rose and the right signs were sent, the colonists, crowded below the peak, knew that on this their founding day they were the center of the god's attention and that in time to come he would attend them, whenever and as long as he was rightly summoned.

Next, to plant the best of their old lives together in the ground of their new, they filed past the pit, casting into it the first fruits of the yield of their former homes and on top of these handfuls of earth they had brought with them. We found the pit dug out almost to the bottom by treasure seekers. What they had left in the last few inches above the floor was a powdery black deposit, soft and sooty, which under the microscope and upon analysis proved to be naturally carbonized vegetable matter. Finally the ancient ritual of plowing the boundary, however it may have been accomplished on the rocky hillside, enclosed the town with its magic circle of furrow and ridge. It evoked as well the town's fertility and prosperity, as it enacted the penetration of mother earth by the bronze plowshare and by the coupling of harnessed bull and heifer. Cosa's life had begun.[3]

The Commissioners and their staff stayed on until they had seen the colony well on its way to self-determination and then laid down their office. Their first business, no doubt, was the allocation of farmlands in the territory and house plots in the town. The parcels of farmland were assigned by drawing lots with the surveyors standing by to record the owner's names in their registers of freeholds, to lead them to their plots, and to walk the boundaries with them. It is clear that the vast majority of freeholders lived on their farms. Our surface surveys of the territory have turned up more than 130 farm sites, almost all of which have yielded evidence of buildings, whereas no evidence of village settlements has come to light. Only those whose farms clustered close to Cosa and, perhaps, to Old Cosa in the lagoon lived in town.[4]

It was to these that the house plots within the walls were allo-

cated. Our excavations have shown that these plots, at least in the
blocks of normal width, were strips running through each block
from street to street. The ratio of their dimensions was one to four
and they were of a size to accommodate a house and a garden. The
terrain left over from the planned streets and public spaces was sufficient for only about 300 such plots of 2,955 square feet (275.00
square m.) each. They would have housed some 1,100 townspeople.
These must have been chiefly engaged in professions, trades, or
crafts, letting their nearby holdings to tenant farmers, presumably
dispossessed Etruscan peasants. The town had been designed to serve
all the colonists as their market place, their center of worship and
self-government, and as their refuge. Its ample public spaces were
for all; its private spaces reserved for only a few.

This distribution of the population determined the next step in
the organization of the community: its subdivision into voting districts on the model of the thirty-three Roman tribes of that time. As
we shall see, there is archaeological evidence which suggests that,
whether they were called *tribus* or *curiae,* wards, they were originally
three in number, one of which will have been prevailingly urban.
They were the voting units, in which the citizens would elect their
magistrates, pass their laws, and ratify their decisions. For the time
being, however, it was for the Commissioners to appoint the first
magistrates, *praetors* or *consuls* and senators, and to promulgate the
basic laws, under which the colony would govern itself, until such
time as they were amended or superseded to suit local conditions.
These statutes and the surveyors' map of the territory, with its
physical features, its grid, and allocations would be posted for all to
consult, while copies would be filed in Rome.[5]

These were the essential preliminaries to the colonists' long and
trying labor of building their city. It would task them for many a year
ahead. Given Cosa's exposed position on the frontier, the prime and
urgent requisite was fortification. Solid houses, proper temples, and
public buildings could wait. The colony must first be protected—the
gods would make allowances. The colonists were not without help
since the military architect-engineers, who had laid out the trace of the
wall were still at hand and among them stonemasons from the hills of
Latium, skilled in working the hard, refractory limestone. They

would train local stonecutters to quarry, dress, and lay the ponderous, irregular blocks. The wall had been designed in the Latin tradition, unlike anything to be seen in Etruria, but resembling, for example, the walls of Norba and Alba Fucens (fig. 14). Like her town plan, Cosa's wall was simply more regular and more finished, except that its design had been affected by Rome's recent contacts with Greek fortifications in Magna Graecia. This was the first and only attempt to graft on to a Roman wall of polygonal masonry a regular Greek system of towers. It displays a concrete example of the continual tug between Roman conservatism and innovation (figs. 15 and 16).

The wall itself, exclusive of the towers, was the common type of towerless, revetment-wall, built up from the slope, below the interior ground level, and filled in behind. The field face, as of any retaining wall, was battered, rising from its base, twenty-six to thirty-three feet (8.00–10.25 m.) to the wall-walk, six feet (1.80 m.) wide. The inner face normally stood only seven to ten feet (2.00–3.00 m.) above grade. The gateways and postern conform, projecting inward from the face of the wall, as though they revetted the passage through an earthwork. No two were quite alike, but they were perfect examples of the Italic, inner-court gateway. Outer and inner gates enclosed a vantage court to trap the enemy who had broken in. Details reflect recent Greek innovations. The outer gates were arched and closed by portcullises.

The tower system (fig. 17) was cautiously designed only to cover the gates and the northwest, west, and southeast fronts, where the approaches were less difficult and visible. It excluded the northern bulge and the eastern salient as unassailable in the traditional sense. The towers, planned and built, were spaced, according to Greek practice, at intervals of effective bowshot, on the average 100 feet (30 m.) apart. Each was square, about 23 feet (6.80 m.) on a side and astride the curtains. Of the two towers designed to flank the northwest gate and the two at the south angle of the wall only the inner projections were actually constructed.

The wall with its gates was laid up from a solid footing course in two faces of large, dry-laid limestone blocks and was packed between with waste rock and spalls. The blocks of the inner face were left unworked as they came from the quarry. The outer face displayed tightly jointed, polygonal masonry that tended toward trapezoidal shapes and was dressed smooth with the point. The visible faces of the towers were finished in the same fashion and the interiors were solidly filled up to the wall-walk.[6]

The laborious operation of fitting each irregular polygon precisely to the next and of tooling the whole exterior surface uniformly produced a striking contrast between the outside and the inside of the wall. The care taken with the exterior manifests the aesthetic or, better, magical value attributed to the wall's outward appearance. With its smooth web of joints the face of the wall represented the impregnability of the living rock from which it rose, daunting the aggressor.

The wall-walk atop the curtains would have been crowned with battlements, as the towers were with upper chambers, pierced for loopholes and embrasures. Traces of chambers have been found on Towers 9 and 10, consisting of the floors and the lower courses of walls. Elsewhere the tumbled remains lie at the foot of the curtains. Both battlements and chambers were built of smaller squared blocks of limestone, and limestone voussoirs arched the doorways opening on the wall-walk.[7]

The stone required for all this was quarried from the hilltop as close as possible to where it was to be employed. These quarries encircled the wall except on the precipitous slopes below its eastern salient. They not only produced an estimated eighty to ninety thousand tons of limestone, but created barriers against attack. They formed rough, irregular scarps of varying heights along virtually all of the towered segments up to the very foot of the wall, and it was this that aborted the completion of the four unfinished towers by removing the rock upon which they had been designed to stand.

The wall was built simultaneously in separate segments, which have left lines of cleavage where they abutted, but was a remarkably homogeneous structure, betraying practically no deviation from a standard of material and techniques. This suggests haste, close supervision, and an uninterrupted campaign of construction. Soundings in the graded fills, laid down along the inside of the wall after it was completed, yielded datable fragments of pottery. None seems to have been made later than the first quarter of the third century. In short, it is safe to assume that the wall was defensible by the end of the colony's first decade, the decade that ended with the outbreak of Rome's first war with Carthage.[8]

It must be added that, probably during the same decade, the town of Old Cosa in the lagoon was also fortified. The tip of the peninsula (fig. 18) was enclosed by a limestone wall of polygonal masonry, bearing every characteristic, except towers, of the wall of the colony (fig. 19). To the naked eye, the stone looks identical with that quarried on the hilltop, but it might have been brought from Mount Argentario. The blocks have the same shape and sizes and are joined and finished after the same fashion. The trace on three sides ran along the water in rectilinear segments. The landward front is no longer extant. The perimeter would probably have measured about 1 1/5 mile (1.93 km.), some one-third longer than Cosa's. The absence of towers was dictated by the site, a sand spit. The wall had to be supported on piles of oak and pine, but these could not have carried the load of towers projecting into the lagoon.[9]

The fortifying of Old Cosa, apparently to protect a larger population than that of New Cosa, raises the question of its status and inhabitants. Had the colonists taken over the old site for themselves? Had the old inhabitants simply been taken into the colony as citizens of full or inferior status? Were the two communities dwelling side by side? The last alternative provides perhaps the best justification for the larger area within the walls.

Just inside the northwest gate of New Cosa an open square was bounded on the northeast by one of the collecting tanks for rainwater and on the southwest side by a large building which seems to have been erected in close connection with the gate (fig. 20). It stood on a terrace, supported by massive retaining walls, still standing up to twenty-three feet (7.00 m.) above the square. Their limestone blocks, polygonal and trapezoidal, their jointing and their finish are indistinguishable from those of the wall. The building on top is poorly preserved and has only been partly investigated. Nevertheless, one can make out most of the general plan. It was entered, well up the southeast side, through a wide gateway, reached by a ramp and opening on a long, narrow courtyard. Broad porticoes bordered either side. Along the ends and behind the opposite portico ran a row of larger and smaller rooms. The whole suggests a warehouse or market into which carts could be driven up the ramp and into the courtyard. The building awaits thorough excavation but can be identified provisionally as the public storehouse, *horreum,* used first for the provisions brought up to tide the colonists over their first winter and then for the stock of supplies held in reserve for times of want or blockade. Its proximity to the terminus of the road from Portus Herculis may further suggest that the supplies brought from Rome came by sea.[10]

These early years, before Rome's deepening involvement in the war with Carthage had drawn off the energies of the colony, also saw the beginnings of the development of the Forum square. These first steps were evidently prompted by at least three immediate necessities. One was the need for providing a more abundant supply of water for the crowds of people and animals that congregated on market days, another for establishing an adjacent precinct for the regular and special assemblies of the citizens, together with a covered hall for the deliberations of the senate. Still another was the need for setting aside and demarcating a part of the square for the voting assemblies of all the citizens.

It will be recalled that the Forum square had been laid out in such a way that its long axis coincided with Street 6, from the northwest gate, and its short axis with Street P, from the Arx (see p. 10). These alignments, however, failed to center it within the larger area, bounded by Streets O and R and Streets 5 and 7, which, as a boundary stone found on the edge of Street 7 attests, had been reserved as public property for the eventual expansion of the civic center. The square came to lie nearer Streets O and 7 than Streets 5 and R. Owing to its gentle northward pitch, its north corner was its lowest point and its east corner, at the foot of the eastern height, its highest.[11]

Three new rock-cut tanks of elongated rectangular proportions were situated around the square (fig. 21). One, perpendicular to its southwest side, collected the rainwater which flowed down Street P. The other two were parallel to either end of the northeast side and impounded the runoff from the eastern height and from the square itself. Between these two, on the short axis of the square, facing the Arx, rose the assembly place and the senate house, the Comitium and Curia, respectively.

The Comitium took the form of an all but square precinct, within which a circular amphitheater of steps was inscribed (fig. 22). The stout walls of the enclosure retained the fill of layers of broken stone and clay that supported the steps. A wide opening and revetted passage led through from the Forum square to the central circular floor. Its concrete pavement left bare at the center a disc of leveled rock, upon which a round base or altar would have stood. The retaining wall was built of mortared slabs of the hard, light-gray-brown sandstone, quarried nearby from the lithified pleistocene dunes behind the later coastline. The curvilinear steps were accurately cut, finished and jointed from the fine-grained, gray-violet tufa brought down the lagoon from the region of Vulci. Only a sector of the two lower steps was found in situ, but, from the height of the retaining wall, 2.66 meters, nine Roman feet, it is evident that eight steps were intended. Examination of the supporting fill indicated that there had been a pause in laying the steps at the level of the third, where a firm, trodden floor had formed before work was resumed.

Centered on the back of the Comitium and raised above its retaining wall stood the Curia. All that remains of the original building are portions of its basement: the concrete floor, the plaster on the outside of the retaining wall, and the traces of two piers that supported the floor above. Nevertheless, the extent of the floor and one edge are enough to show that the plan and dimensions of the building were approximately the same as its successor's. The absence of other remains would seem to imply that this first Curia was a lightly built, temporary structure, probably of sun-dried brick, to be replaced when circumstances permitted. It was probably a makeshift, rectangular hall, about twenty by thirty Roman feet on the interior, with its floor on a level with the top step of the Comitium.[12]

The design, at least, was both simple and sophisticated (fig. 23). It combined an auditorium of central plan open to the sky, where attention would have been drawn to the speaker in the center, with a strong, axial tension between the entry passage and the gabled facade of the hall above. Attention would be shifted when a magistrate emerged to make a pronouncement, converting the rotunda to a nave. The ultimate source of the plan was undoubtedly the Roman custom of standing in the ancient Comitium at Rome, which was laid out on a gentle, assymetrically curving slope, crowned by its Curia. The rounding of the loose, theatral form into a geometric expression of citizen unanimity under executive guidance was perhaps inspired by Greek or West Greek experiments with circular assembly places. Two other Latin colonies, Alba Fucens and Paestum—Cosa's twin—built similar comitia. Both were much larger than Cosa's and, according to their excavators, erected some fifty or more years later.[13]

The surveyors who laid out the boundaries of the larger area around the Forum square seem not to have taken into consideration the advantages of the sunny, southwest exposure or the size of the buildings that were likely to be placed along this side of the square. Be that as it may, the architect of the Comitium and Curia, although his design was as compact as possible, found that the space of only fifty-odd feet (15.00 m.) between the square and Street 7 was far too short for his building. Part of the Comitium and all of the Curia had to lie outside the boundary. The street was blocked but continued on either side. This would not be the last time that zoning boundaries were disregarded.

It was the southeast end of the Forum square, beyond the Comitium, that was reserved for the stated assemblies of the whole citizen body, mustered in its military and territorial subdivisions. This necessitated leveling on either side where the rocky foot of the eastern height and the gentle slope from the Arx intruded on the square. The rock was cut back vertically, leaving level shelves, into which were hewn four corresponding rectangular pits along both sides. They were sizable cavities, roughly 3 by 6 Roman feet with a depth of 3 to 3½ feet. Each was framed by an accurately dressed band for the bedding of curb stones. Around one of the pits these were found in place, while a handsbreadth of loam, left covering its floor, still held the traces of the carbonized rootlets of a fair-sized tree. The first in each row of these planting boxes was centered on the line of the southeast side of the Comitium, and the last fell just short of the end of the square. The three intervals between, marked by the trees and seen from either side, made as many parallel courses, stretching across the breadth of the square (fig. 24). They would not only distinguish this end of the square from the other but signal the lanes in which the three subdivisions of the citizenry lined up in the Roman way to cast their unit votes. The trees, too, would have shaded through the day the officials who verified credentials at one end of the line and tallied the voice votes at the other.

The structures we have reviewed document the vigor and persistence which marked the start of the colony. But, already in the unfinished steps of the Comitium and the provisional Curia, one can detect the drag of the long and exhausting war with its burden of loss and disruption. It is symptomatic that work on the retaining wall of the Arx that fronted the Forum had stopped shortly after it had begun in conjunction with the building of Tower 14 and that the high place remained an open precinct with an altar covering the foundation pit. At least within the area of our excavations no trace of substantial, stone-built houses of this period have been found. It is also indicative that Cosa struck her own coins in two issues, one apparently at the inception of the colony, the other considerably later, probably after the war. Again, the paucity of imported tableware seems to indicate that the colonists made do with what they had brought with them from Rome or what the local potters could provide.

With the end of the war, in 241, Cosa could begin to regain the lost momentum. Work could be resumed gradually in the Forum and on the Arx. Here the retaining and enclosing walls seem to have been taken in hand again, but more significantly, the long-deferred Temple of Jupiter was erected (fig. 25). Its site was the rocky shoulder just below the sacred square, which fell away west-southwestward to the wall. Of the building itself nothing remains but its outlines, marked on the rock by the beds worked for the seating of its podium and foundations. The temple faced north-northwestward across the town and the lagoon, past Old Cosa to Telamon. One side loomed across the water from Portus Herculis; the other flanked the augur's position in his *templum* without interfering with his field of vision. The plan, an elongated version of the normal, single-cella temple of the day, was evidently designed to fit the narrow site. Its long cella and deep pronaos made the most of the shoulder. The conformation of its northern declivity furnished a foundation for a central stairway, rising from the rockbound platform below, where the altar stood.

This temple was eventually demolished when its grander successor was built. The god and his image was incorporated into the new temple and with him all of the decorative elements of his old house, in accordance with the law of the conservation of sacred matter. These were the terracotta simas and filigreed cresting, the antefixes, eaves tiles and revetments of the wooden roof and entablature. Some were buried under floors, some built into walls, and others reused in their proper places. Having these, we have been able to raise the ghost of the old temple and deck it anew (fig. 26). While its plan and, presumably, its structure were typical of Latin temples, these painted moldings in low relief are outstanding examples of the early Hellenistic style in central Etruria. More precisely, each of them has its counterpart in Tarquinia. There can be no doubt that they were made there, and not long after 240 B.C. Cosa, at this stage, being without the artisans to shape and mold such finery, turned to a nearby Etruscan workshop.[14]

Before the resumption of work on the Comitium and Curia, the public tank to the southeast was enclosed by a wall or parapet at least 3½ feet high. This appears to have been less a measure of public safety than a design to limit the use of the water to the building operations. The enclosure extended beyond the northwest end of the tank up to the retaining wall of the Comitium. Here it was graded up with a fill of broken stone and earth to the level that had previously been reached at the third step, leaving a wide opening into the Comitium. A narrower opening in the northeast side of the enclosure made it accessible to the other end of the building yard.

The Comitium and Curia were now given permanent form (fig. 27). While the steps of the former were being completed in stone, the temporary hall was torn down and its basement replaced by a massive substructure, straight from the school of the builders of the town wall. Like the wall, its exposed faces were battered, since it had a retaining as well as a supporting function. Though built with somewhat smaller blocks, more regularly coursed, the fitting and finishing was impeccably the same. The space enclosed by the rough inner faces was filled as they rose by layer upon layer of clay, waste stone, and chips of tufa from the steps. The new hall that stood on the podium has left no traces except its approximate dimensions. We can be sure that it was rebuilt solidly with limestone and mortar. If, as one must suppose, its model was the Curia in Rome, it would have seated some sixty persons on the low steps along the side walls with the presiding magistrates and two or three clerks on the dais at the back. The capacity of the Comitium's completed amphitheater would have been about six hundred. Paestum's held twelve hundred. Whereas the senators were of standing, relatively well-to-do, and ambitious, the assembled citizens would have been those who got their livelihood in or about the town or simply happened to be on hand. As in Rome, ordinary day-by-day political activity was the game of those whose business brought them to the city or kept them there.

The arrangements for voting and mustering in the southeastern part of the Forum also received attention (fig. 28). In the intervals between trees, pairs of smaller pits were chiseled out of the rock, 2 Roman feet square, 2¼ feet deep, and set 10 feet apart. These also were framed by chases for the bedding of curbstones having, however, lateral projections on either side (fig. 29). Pits of these dimensions would be too small for trees but not too large for posts, their size being determined by the space occupied by a crouching workman wielding chisel and hammer. Chocks would be needed, but the projections of the curbs look as though they might have been designed to step braces holding a post upright. Placed as they were, the pairs would suggest support of light, bracketed roofs or awnings, the better to protect the officials from the elements.

The regained momentum was interrupted in 225 by the last concerted Gallic raid on Roman territory and by the extraordinary mobilization of Roman manpower it provoked. Some 70,000 marauding Gauls reached the vicinity of Cosa before they were turned back by the converging Roman forces. The battle in which they were annihilated between two Roman armies was fought in the fields east of Telamon only ten miles (16 km.) away. Cosa, it seems, did not suffer except for the alarm, a foretaste of what was to come when Hannibal crossed the Alps seven years later.[15]

We can place in the succeeding decade of Rome's desperate straits another and enigmatic structure connected with the Comitium. The enclosure around the southeast tank had served its purpose.

The northwest end of it, beyond the tank, was now transformed into a temporary platform behind the blocked-up low-level opening into the assembly place (fig. 29). The area was floored with roof tiles. Its walls were given a coat of plaster and a cover joint at the floor. A flight of stairs, made of sun-dried bricks, led up to the south corner of the Comitium (fig. 30). A roughly carved drum of limestone was set on the floor as an altar. It would appear that these arrangements were hastily contrived to accommodate persons who had official business with the assembly or the senate, giving the platform the semblance of the more permanent Graecostasis which bordered the Comitium at Rome and had a similar function.[16]

During the brief existence of this counterpart, a thin layer of caked mud covered the floor and twelve bronze coins that had been dropped on it. The markings on one coin were illegible. The rest of the coins had been struck between the first and last quarters of the century. Four were of various Roman mintage. Three came from Punic Sardinia's last years and one each from Cosa, Naples, Syracuse, and Marseilles. This teasing assortment would represent the small change of Cosa itself, before the Roman *denarius* and its prow-bronze prevailed, or that of any other maritime town on the Tyrrhenian coast. It would also attest to the presence of emissaries from these parts, perhaps just before but more likely just after the outbreak of the second war with Carthage. One cannot help remembering the councils of the thirty Latin colonies, deliberations that, after the disastrous reverses and the exhausting drain on the resources of the Commonwealth, divided the Latins in 209 into the twelve faithless and the eighteen steadfast. Of the latter, in Livy's list, the men of Ponza, Paestum, and Cosa together represented the group along the Tyrrhenian shore. As Livy put it, these were among the colonies "by whose support, at that moment, the dominion of the Roman people stood firm."[17]

Notes

1. G. Tibiletti, "La politica agraria dalla guerra annibalica ai Gracchi," *Athenaeum* n. s. 28 (1950): 22–232. Cohorts, *vexilla*: Cicero, *Phil* 2. 102; *Leg. Agr.* 2. 86; Plutarch, *C. Gracchus* 11.

2. F. E. Brown, "Cosa I: History and Topography," *MAAR* 20 (1951):

113. E. T. Salmon, *Roman Colonization under the Republic* (London, 1969), p. 38, prefers 4000. Calculated population after A. Afzelius, *Die römischen Eroberung Italians* ("Acta Jutlandica," aarschrift for AArhus Universitet, 14, 3, Copenhagen, 1942), p. 100 f.

3. Varro, *Ling.* 7. 8–9; *Tabulae Iguvinae* VI a, 1–22. Cf. E. Norden, "Aus altrömischer Priesterbücher," *Skrifter Kungl. Humanistika Vetenskapfundet i Lund"* 29 (1939): 3–90; K. Latte, "Augur und Templum in der Varronische Augurformel," *Philologus* 97 (1948): 143–59. Festus, 310 L; Ovid, Fast, 4, 820–25; Plutarch, *Romulus* 11. Varro, *Ling.* 5. 142. Cf. in general J. Le Gall, "Rites de fondation," *Studi sulla città antica* (Bologna, 1970), pp. 59–65; J. Rykwert, *The Idea of a Town* (Princeton, 1976), pp. 44–48, 65–68, 84–91, 121–26, 132–35.

4. A. Rudorff, *Die Schriften die römischen Feldmesser,* vol. 2 (Berlin, 1852), pp. 366–69; Salmon, *Roman Colonization under the Republic,* pp. 24 f., 168, n. 27; O. A. W. Dilke, *The Roman Land Surveyors* (Newton Abbot, 1971), p. 96 f. S. L. Dyson, "Settlement Patterns in the Ager Cosanus," *NSc* (forthcoming): 14–18.

5. E. Kornemann, "Coloniae," *RE* 4 (1901): 571,577. F. Castagnoli, "Le 'formae' delle colonie romane e le miniature dei codici dei gromatici," *MemLinc* ser. 7, 4 (1943): 83–118.

6. F. E. Brown, "Cosa I: History and Topography," *MAAR* 20 (1951): 28–49; G. Lugli, *La Tecnica edilizia romana* (Rome, 1957), vol. 1, pp. 111–15.

7. The similar mortared masonry of the inner cross-walls of the gates is bonded into the polygonal masonry of the side walls, *pace* A. von Gerkan, "Zur Datierung der Kolonie Cosa," *Miscellanea Libertini* (Florence, 1958), pp. 151 f.

8. Brown, "Cosa I: History and Topography," *MAAR* 20 (1951): 49–57.

9. M. Santangelo, *L'antiquarium di Orbetello* (Rome, 1954), pp. 38–42. P. Raveggi, "Sulla costruzione delle mura etrusche di Orbetello," *StEtr* 7 (1933): 413–15.

10. Vide chap. I, p. 10.

11. Vide chap. 1, p. 22.

12. L. Richardson Jr., "Cosa and Rome, Comitium and Curia," *Archaeology* 10 (1957): 49–55; J. A. Hanson, *Roman Theater-Temples* (Princeton, 1959), pp. 37–39; L. R. Taylor, *Roman Voting Assemblies* (Ann Arbor, 1966), pp. 21–23.

13. J. Mertens, *Alba Fucens,* vol. 1 (Brussels, 1969), pp. 98–101; C. Krause, "Zur baulichen Gestalt des republikanischen Comitiums," *RömMitt* 83 (1976): 31–69.

14. L. Richardson Jr., "Cosa II: The Temples of the Arx," *MAAR* 26 (1960): 151–69. Cf. M. Torelli, "Terza campagna di scavo a punta della Vipera (S. Marinella)," *StEtr* 35 (1968): 342–46. On the edge of an eaves or sima-tile (CB613) its place on the roof was marked by two incised Etruscan letters.

15. Polybius, 2. 25–31; P. Sommella, "Antichi campi di battaglia in Italia," *Quaderni dell'Istituto di Topografia Antica della Università di Roma* 3 (1967): 9–34.

16. Varro, *Ling.* 5, 155. E. Gjerstad, "Il Comizio Romano dell'età republicana," *Acta Instituti Romani Regni Sueciae* 5 (1941): 105 f., 144 f.; Krause, "Zur baulichen Gestalt des republikanischen Comitiums,"*RömMitt* 83 (1976): 40 f.

17. Coins: CF 2224, 2227–31, 2233–37 (nos. 2, 5, 9, 15, 17, 18, 19, 25, 26, 27, 28) in T. V. Buttrey, "Cosa: The Coins," *MAAR* 34 (1980): 16, 21f., 45. Livy,

27. 9. 7–10, 10. 10; A. J. Toynbee, *Hannibal's Legacy,* vol. 1 (London, 1965) 90 f., 111–13.

III: The Forum

The crucial year, 209 B.C., that split the thirty Latin colonies into two camps, was also the turning point of the war. While it dragged on for six more years in the south and north of Italy, the central regions were no longer directly affected. Cosa, despite the continuous, heavy demand on its manpower, could use its favored position on the supply line to Spain to begin restoring its economy. These latter years of the war consequently saw a modest resumption of building activity along the northeast side of the Forum square.

The makeshift platform beside the Comitium was made permanent and floored at a higher level. For the deity, whose altar had stood there, an open precinct was raised behind and above it, extending to the boundary line of Street 7 (fig. 31). The fill underneath its floor yielded a freshly minted *triens* of the newly issued sextantal standard. The old altar was piously preserved in the substructure of the stairs that led to the consecrated enclosure, but the new altar has left no trace. The deity, however, is likely to have been Concordia, who represented the power that bound like-minded men together. The goddess first manifested herself in the political strife of fourth-century Rome, where she had her shrine beside the Comitium. A dedication, suiting her epiphany at Cosa, was found reused in fragments nearby (fig. 32). It was she who would have prompted the Cosans to be of one mind with the other loyal Latins, and her continued presence would keep them in concord.[1]

At about the same time, a building of a very different sort was under construction at the south corner of the square (figs. 33 and 34). It was a strongly but roughly built rectangular structure with mortared walls three feet thick, pierced by a single doorway, which opened, not from the Forum, but from Street 7. The interior, ten by twenty-five Roman feet, was covered by a stone vault and divided by a two-foot wall into unpaved, outer and inner rooms. A vaulted cellar under the southeast half of the floor was accessible through a square manhole, closed by a stone lid. The building, in sum, gives every appearance of a jail, in the Roman sense of a place of detention for malefactors awaiting trial or execution. With its heavily built, vaulted chambers and underground oubliette, it seems a rectilinear copy of the *carcer* and *Tullianum* of Rome. Livy implies that every city-state had a jail, and Vitruvius prescribes that it adjoin the Forum. Oddly enough, Cosa's *carcer* seems to be the only one that has been identified outside Rome.[2]

The space between these two buildings was now remodeled to form an enlarged forecourt for the platform and the Sacellum of Concordia, overlooking the voting place in the square (fig. 35). The open tank was covered by a stone vault. Its temporary enclosure on the northeast and southeast was razed to the foundations and replaced by walls skirting Street 7 and the end of the jail. The enclosed area was leveled up, paved with concrete and given access by a flight of steps from the square.

Once the war had ended triumphantly in 201, the Latin colonies which felt their losses most acutely began to petition the Roman senate for fresh drafts of colonists. Cosa was third in line. The senate, hard put to find recruits and having more urgent priorities, rejected her first petition in 199. Two years later a second embassy was ordered to enroll a thousand, provided none of them had sided with the invader. The cost of Cosa's fidelity was the implied loss of two-fifths of her citizens. Not all were casualties. Some, it appears, who fought in Spain, chose to settle there. Others drifted to Rome. The senate's reliance on the discretion of the Cosans in selecting their new colonists was an exceptional mark of trust, but the stipulation warned them that Rome would scrutinize the list. Cosa was authorized to draw volunteers from anywhere in the war-weary Commonwealth. Her prospects were good. The colony by this time was no longer an outpost on the frontier. It was securely established and dominant in its Etruscan neighborhood. The promise of material, social, and political betterment in a free city-state, broadly based as it was on agriculture, fishing, and commerce would be attractive. In any event it is plain that Rome's confidence was justified.[3]

We know little or nothing about the individual colonists, except, as we shall see, that they added two more voting units to the old three (see p. 41).[4] What our excavations show is that their arrival sparked a burst of building and rebuilding that lasted through the century and changed the face of the town and countryside. With it go the unmistakable signs of thriving, local crafts and trades. Subsidies, perhaps, from Rome, bounty from the wars, and the growing prosperity of the colony fueled the revival. It appears so sweeping and so incessant that it defies a strictly chronological account. It is first manifested in the Forum.

Except for the siting of the Comitium and Curia on the short axis of the square between the symmetrical tanks, there had been no indication of a predetermined plan for the use of the public land bounded by Streets O and R, 5 and 7. The various buildings stretching southeastward from the Comitium had sprung up haphazardly one by one as they were needed, becoming more or less permanent fixtures along the choicer side of the square. Now, shortly after the reinforcement of the colony, a master design for the enclosure of the other three sides of the square was undertaken (figs. 36 and 37). It comprised eight similar buildings, unitary in function, running back from the square to the bounding streets: four, in two pairs, on the southwest side, separated by an open space, opposite the Comitium; two at either end, flanking the avenues leading to the square. Because of the eccentricity of the square within the surrounding tract, the buildings along the side and both ends varied in depth, but the separate part of each building that gave onto the square was practically identical with the others. The master plan also called for porticoes in front of their facades on all three exposures, leaving free the remainder of the northeast side for an eventual public building of importance.

Of these eight buildings covering about 1¼ acres (½ hect.), only one, beside the north corner of the square, has been completely excavated (fig. 38). Its counterpart beside the south corner has been explored by a number of sounding trenches sufficient to demonstrate that the plan of its Forum end was essentially the same. The facades of the others on the square have been exposed outside and in, and their main walls along the streets and within have been traced at ground level. Other soundings have tested their floors and the stratified layers between and beneath them. Allowing for irregularities in construction and differences due to the lay of the land, rising southwestward and falling at either end, the outlines of each are legible, and the particulars of the north and south buildings help to elucidate the others.

Each building presented to the square a tripartite facade composed of the high, central opening of a vestibule admitting to the interior, flanked by the wide doorways of two sizable shops. The doorways, in their original form, were divided by columnar supports, of which two foundations and five or six capitals have been found. The interior behind the shops took the shape of atrium halls with lateral wings, *alae,* at the back and a room on either side. Each atrium had its open skylight, shallow catch basin, and rainwater cistern. These units, arranged as mirror images, were common to each pair of buildings which otherwise were treated diversely.

The two buildings between the northwest end of the square and Street O were shortest (fig. 39). The smaller room of each atrium unit was turned outward to give on the avenue between them, and beside each a second vestibule and entrance were opened. Both buildings were completed by ranges of shops at a lower level on the street. These spaces, to judge by the northeast building, were planned to accommodate four shops each, three of which were, in this case, partitioned off during construction.

The four buildings along the southwest side were a little more than double the depth of their units facing the square (fig. 40). The pair toward the southeast end, where the rise of the terrain was slight, gave evidence of having repeated the same unit plan facing Street 5, with four large shops and two vestibules. The floors of the other pair toward the northwest end, where the slope was steeper, lay 6 to 8½ feet (1.80–2.50 m.) below the level of the street. Their rooms had been cut back in the rising rock, in order that they communicate through the party walls with their units facing the square, whose plan, however, they did not repeat. The space between the two pairs of buildings was treated as an appendage of the Forum square. It was leveled and paved with concrete from wall to wall. Its upper end on Street 5 was closed off except for a central opening above a short, three-sided flight of steps. At its lower end on the square a second flight of stairs passed through a free-standing, bicolumnar gateway, whose chunky Tuscan bases were found in place. The paved surface overlaid a long stone-vaulted cistern on either side. One was the old open tank of the first years of the colony (see p. 22), the other a newly made counterpart.

The two buildings at the southeast end of the square were the longest by a few feet. They were also the most dilapidated, having been used as quarries for building stone in later times. To their normal atrium units there seem to have been added ranges of rooms across the back. Separate from these and at a lower level, there are traces of rows of two-room shops, giving on Street R, probably eight in all.

These eight utilitarian buildings reflected the requirements of the daily business of the Forum and at the same time were a source of revenue to the colony. The sixteen commodious shops about the square would have been let to the more substantial artisans and tradesmen of the town. Two or three, at least, of the original tenants were metalsmiths, as their refuse and forges indicate. The tenants of the twenty-odd shops, large or small, single or double, that faced the surrounding streets, supplied most of the colony's commodities, from fine pottery to pitchforks. The eight or ten atrium units, while they displayed the form of the core of a contemporary Roman house, were evidently not designed as dwellings, since they did not include living quarters. They can be defined as adaptations of a typical atrium to public or commercial use.

A clue to the form and purpose of these buildings may be found in ancient writings which referred to scattered buildings in Rome by the proper name of Atrium. One such building was the public record office on the Capitol, predecessor of the Tabularium; another the office and archive of the censors in the Campus Martius; still another was the guild hall of the shoemakers, which was periodically used for religious purposes; a fourth was an auction hall, while the fifth and sixth, along with four shops, made room for the Basilica Porcia in 184. The name of all these obviously implies that their common characteristic was an atrium, and all were, in one sense or another, places of public business and resort. Their common designation seems to record a stage in Roman architecture when the central space of the house—ample, covered except for its source of light, uncluttered by supports—was adapted to a wide range of public uses. Where none of these buildings has survived, the Atria around the Forum of Cosa may give a glimpse of what they were like, and, conversely, the Roman Atria may suggest the varied functions which the Cosan Atria served.[5]

The open space between the buildings on the southwest side of the square not only preserved and emphasized the visual link between the square and the Arx up and down Street P, but presumably had its own utilitarian place in the master plan. The function of the open space bordered by the cisterns must have been closely connected with the abundant supply of water provided by the two cisterns, each almost a hundred feet (30.00 m.) long, one of which was created on purpose. The stairs and gateway on Street 5, while they served the public, were also on the shortest line of communication, via the southeast gate, between the Forum and the lagoon and anchorage down below. A paved area, close to the sources of fresh fish, mollusks, and crustaceans, with the means at hand to keep them alive and succulent, describes an outdoor fish market, which Cosa certainly would not have lacked. Noting that Rome's fish market at the time adjoined one side of its Forum, I would suggest that the appendage to Cosa's square was its *forum piscarium*. The two-column monument that set it off from the square may well have honored the public-spirited citizen who donated it.[6]

These unadorned, utilitarian buildings were erected according to uniform specifications, following the current practice in the construction of houses, and similar to those applied in the temporary platform beside the Comitium. They were founded directly on the rock and bed-soil, which bore no trace of previous buildings. A rough foundation course and wall bases of squared blocks of limestone, laid in clay, supported walls of sun-dried brick (fig. 38). Doorways, corners, and intersections were quoined and bonded with larger blocks. Coats of plaster covered and preserved them from the elements. Dry-laid masonry and lime mortar were as yet used only for walls that were expected to last forever, walls of temples of the gods and of the institutions of the city.

The construction of each building was assigned to two or more gangs of workmen, as indicated by the vertical seams where the stints of two gangs met. Signs of haste and carelessness—walls out of line, inaccurate dimensions—are many. Pressure from outside for immediate occupancy can be detected in the fills in front of the buildings along the northwest end, where the natural surface of the ground dipped. Here it is evident that the shops had been let and were in use before the square was finally leveled and the porticoes added. Each occupant had laid a temporary apron of rammed earth or concrete in front of his doorway, while he waited for the pavement of the portico.

The coins found under the original floors of the buildings at either end of the square were all of the first issues of the *denarius* and sextantal bronze, probably struck during the last decade of the third century. The discarded potsherds from the same contexts can independently be referred to its last quarter. On the other hand the continuous sequence of building operations indicates that, some time after the end of the first decade of the second century, work on the master plan came to a momentary halt when more urgent projects intervened.[7]

The first of these projects was the enlargement of the Curia (fig. 37). The hall, in which the town-fathers met, had not been planned for expansion. The sessions of eighty or ninety years would have produced a bulky accumulation of rolls of records and documents, which would have had to be shelved in the room, progressively reducing its available space. The members, to judge by Roman practice, were accustomed to circulate freely and crowding would have posed serious problems: voting was usually by division; the doors opened inward, and privileged persons, like the sons of senators, were invited to observe the proceedings from the entrance end. Perhaps an ancient version of Parkinson's law was at work to multiply clerks and attendants. In any event, it was decided to add a room on either side of the Curia by simply extending its back wall and the side walls of the Comitium. The resulting rooms were relatively long and narrow but added about one and one half the previous space. Supplementary rooms of this sort had already been included in the plans of the curiae of Alba Fucens and Paestum. At Cosa the two basements, roughly finished and without flooring, were fitted with doors at the back and doubtless served as municipal lumber rooms.[8]

Next, Concordia's precinct was replaced by her temple, flanking the new Curia and facing the square (figs. 41 and 42). It reverently incorporated the foundations of the old Sacellum, marking them by the steps placed above. It rose from the same level as the Curia on a massive substructure of finely wrought, polygonal masonry and equalled the Curia in height. Its plan, twice as long as wide and consisting of a rectangular cella, deep pronaos and prostyle facade of two columns, echoed the Temple of Jupiter on the Arx and was of about the same size. One of the travertine capitals of Tuscan profile, found toppled into the Comitium, gives us the essential dimensions for the elevation and a module for the proportions. The forecourt of the Sacellum was now the temple's and the altar of Concord was moved there, below the temple steps and on the axis of the gateway from the square. More than half of its stone platform has survived.

The molded and painted terracotta plaques that embellished the jutting timbers of the roof were also closely related to the ones on the Temple of Jupiter (fig. 43). Those, as we have seen, had come from a workshop in Tarquinia. The single revetment, the sima and the filigreed cresting of the Temple of Concord display similar geometric designs in a slightly simplified version. A few plaques carefully pressed into their molds and retouched before firing are executed in the distinctive buff clay of Tarquinia. All the rest, as well as the antefixes, were made, much less skillfully, of the red clay of Cosa. It is as if the plaques and antefixes had been modeled and the molds prepared in Tarquinia and brought to Cosa along with samples to go by. Accordingly Cosan artisans may have then been trained by example how to cast them and been left to do the rest.

The gable space on the facade of the temple framed a pedimental composition of half life-size, terracotta figures, represented by some seventy-five fragments. Careful study of these suggests that this depicted the climactic moment of the recognition of young Paris by his parents and family. The Temple of Concord thus adds another to the half-dozen or so pediments of this kind in Hellenistic Etruria, whose somewhat exotic, mythological content seems to have, at least for us, little or no connection with the divinity worshiped. The figures of our pediment, like the others, were modeled freehand and attached from the hips down to heavy terracotta plates for mounting, while above they leaned forward in the round. Although they were made at Cosa of the local clay, they can hardly have been the work of the local artisans. Like the pediment of nearby Telamon they must have been shaped and fired by practiced Etruscan artists from Tarquinia or Vulci.[9]

The temple harked back to the severe architectural forms of third-century Latium and still depended for its decorations on Etruscan styles and craftsmen. Yet it must have been finished toward the end of the first quarter of the second century. That it followed the enlarged Curia is evident from the fact that the blocks of the podium, where they were hidden by its wall, were left without tight joints or smooth finish. The one legible coin extracted from the heart of the podium was of a third-century issue, and the pottery from soundings under the floors is no later than the early second century. As time went on, numerous sculptural offerings of terracotta, portraying the goddess, and perhaps others, stood in the temple or were affixed to its walls. Ten or so have been identified as life-size, draped female figures, two of which have kept Concordia's attributes, the veiled and diademed head and the cornucopia. Beside these, a fragment of the snout of a half life-size pig recalls the miraculous sow that was the badge of the Latins.[10]

During this interval, while the new buildings along the other three sides of the square were awaiting their porticoes, preparations were in progress for the distribution and impounding of the public reserves of water to be collected from the roofs and spaces above the square. The open tank northwest of the Comitium was now vaulted. In the west corner area, bounded by Streets 5 and O, the large open tank, that had been part of the initial water supply of the town (see p. 11) was renovated and divided by a row of three stout, stone piers to support a vaulted or timber-built covering. The space left between it and the buildings at the corner of the square and the area of the whole north corner bounded by Streets O and 7 appear to have been sold or leased at the time for private use. The latter plot was quickly occupied by two separate double-shops on Street O.

Around 170 B.C. the porticoes were finally erected (fig. 44).

They surrounded the square with a continuous, covered walk along three sides, crossing the entrances at either end and extending as far as Street 7 on the northwest. The southeast portico also served the through pedestrian traffic on Street Q. The concrete floor of the southwest portico with its return at the north corner was raised by two steps above the square. Elsewhere the floors of the porticoes ran level with the square and were curbed between columns. The bays were wide, ideally 18¾ Roman feet (5.55 m.) but somewhat irregular, since they were made to correspond as much as possible with the openings behind.

Of the columns, thirty-six in all, the stumps of ten, the plinths of thirteen and the beds of twelve have survived (figs. 45 and 46). Only one is missing. They were set out 11½ feet (3.40 m.) from the facades. Some were founded directly on the rock in socketed beds, the rest, where the rock dropped off, on monolithic drums of travertine of varying heights, dressed at the top to the setting circles. The shafts, like those of the shop doorways and the Temple of Concord, were built of mortared segments of sandstone slab covered by hard, white plaster, which gave them their lower diameters of 2¼ feet (0.67 m.). The travertine Tuscan capitals were also roughened for plastering. By calculation the columns stood 15 feet (4.45 m.) high, bearing the thick wooden architraves over the broad spans (fig. 47). These, in turn, supported the tiled roofs, overhanging some 5 feet (1.48 m.) to the edges of the gutter channels and covering the steps and walkways under the eaves. Here the crowds at the festive spectacles in the square, be they processions, games, shows, or public funerals, would take their place.

By trimming the rock and filling with chips, the square had been brought to a level with a gently graded descent from south to north. Once the gutters and the other permanent fixtures on its surface were in place, its thick pavement of broken stone and clay could be laid (fig. 48). The gutters, which would also serve as curbs, were composed of long blocks of travertine with a rounded channel down the middle. They were carefully contrived to collect the rainfall from the roofs of the buildings, porticoes, and open catchments. The water was then purified and conveyed underground to the two recently covered reservoirs. The larger of these reservoirs was in the north angle of the area and received, from two settling tanks, the water from the porticoes and buildings on three sides of the square. The rainfall collected along the fourth side and from the Curia and Comitium passed through another settling tank into the smaller reservoir.

The positioning of the gutters in relation to the porticoes and steps along either side of the southeast half of the square required that they overlap the old planting pits and post-sockets. The former were merely reduced in size, but the sockets were abandoned, filled, and paved over. To replace them a new and more elaborate set of pits was hewn out along the gutter at the end of the square (figs. 41 and 44). There were twenty-four in all, placed at the corners of six squares defining five intervals, of which the central was wider than the others. The new pits were somewhat smaller than the old and, instead of curbs, had lids, three of which were found still in place. They were obviously used only on occasion, when presumably they also held posts that could support continuous or discontinuous cover across the end of the square. The intervals between them suggest that five lanes were now needed instead of three, and it follows that the additional files were those of the new colonists, divided into two territorial subdivisions, voting as two units.[11]

The wider central interval might further suggest that the sockets were designed for other occasional uses of the square, one of which might have been the erection of a temporary stage with its dominant central portal. The lidded sockets for the temporary *scaenae frons* in the contemporary theater of Pergamon offer a close, if more elaborate, comparison, while the outdoor festival theaters of contemporary Rome cannot have been very different. Perhaps one should think of this new arrangement as a sort of all-purpose installation, capable, for example, of supporting platforms or bleachers reared against the columns behind them.[12]

Another installation of a different sort was set along the southwest gutter across the short axis of the square. It was a low stone step, about 2½ feet wide and of the same length as the breadth of the Comitium opposite and the fish market behind it (figs. 44 and 49). Some of its well-worn original blocks had been patched or replaced. One end is missing and a part still lies beneath the roots of an olive, but in the remaining, abraded surfaces twenty-odd mortises can be

counted. They were of various shapes and sizes, round, square, rectangular, or rounded at one end. Some, for lack of space, had been
sunk in the adjacent gutter and steps. The existing end block was
smooth, perhaps one of two plinths supporting terminal features.
The two round-ended mortises were symmetrically placed so as to
define a wider central space between two equal end spaces. All the
mortises were evidently fitted by the tenons of upright slabs or pil-
lars, *stelae,* of stone or wood. Some would have been inscribed,
others would have borne inscribed or painted tablets. The two divid-
ing *stelae* were presumably original, the rest erected one after another
from time to time.

Given its central position on the square, this installation can be
identified as the colony's bulletin board which displayed the essential
laws and decrees of permanent public interest, as well as transitory
notices of limited effect. Its three divisions perhaps suggest a princi-
ple of classification. At the same time that the adjacent bays of the
portico were erected, the open spaces on either side of the entrance to
the fish market were blocked up with masonry stuccoed with exceptionally thick and carefully prepared coats of plaster. The finish coat
has survived only at the very bottom, but, since the closing of the
spaces had no structural significance, it is tempting to think that
these surfaces, under cover behind the bulletin board, bore a painted
copy of the *forma* of the colony, the surveyors' map of the territory,
with its old and newly allotted holdings.[13]

During the later stages of the execution of the master plan, the
paving of the streets of the town was in progress, beginning with the
principal thoroughfares around the Forum. With paving went the
construction of the sewage system (fig. 50). Under the pavements of
irregular blocks of limestone between the sidewalks of these arteries
ran the mains leading out through the gates. Across the opening of the
entrance way to the square, facing the busy intersection of Streets O
and 6, the final major element of the plan was erected, a monumental
portal that was framed by the buildings on either side and crowned the
approach from the northwest gate below (figs. 47 and 51). Asserting
the transition between the random world outside and the organized
world of the Forum, it took the shape of a triple archway, composed
of a broad central passage between two narrow ones.

Its carcass, split in two and toppled sideways from the stumps of its piers, still shows its original aspect and dimensions. It was a thickset mass, built of mortared rubble work and arched over wooden centering. The surviving plaster on the surfaces bears the traces of archivolt moldings and of a stringcourse farther up. The impost of the central arch stood just above the crowns of the side arches and its radius was only slightly less. The conduit that conveyed the drip from the northwest portico to its reservoir ran down the southwest side of the entrance way and through a pipe in the pier of the right-hand arch. To accommodate it that pier was built a little wider than its mate on the other side. In front of the middle piers the pavement enframed the beds of two missing rectangular objects, the inside corners of which had been protected by tapered stone fender-blocks. Too long for statue bases or the plinths of columns, they suggest basins instead.

With the archway across one end and the colonnade across the other the entrance way had become a sort of vestibule, both corridor and courtyard, now paved like the streets. Across its long axis, two-thirds of the way from the arch, the paving stones outlined the rectangular foundations of its central feature. The remains of a pair of steps behind it indicate that this was a platform, about 2¼ feet (0.67 m.) high, the size and shape of the familiar judicial tribunal on which a magistrate placed his folding chair to preside at a court session. This one allowed space for the chairs of two counselors as well. If this were its purpose, and no other is likely, we must imagine our ambiguous space converted, on stated days, to an outdoor courtroom, Roman style.[14]

The Forum of Cosa is the only one of its kind that can be visualized as it was planned and built, not because it was unique, but simply because none of the others that resembled it happens to have been resurrected. During the two decades after the crushing of Carthage, while Rome was dismantling the Hellenistic kingdoms, some nineteen Latin and citizen colonies were founded in Italy. We can rest assured that each had a Forum, presumably planned by the colonial office in Rome. This was the period when the first heady impact of Hellenistic architecture was felt in Rome and Italy and when Roman architects were stimulated both to imitate and innovate, as they began to create the forms and techniques of a new imperial Roman architecture. The master plan of the Forum of Cosa belongs in this context, which is succinctly recorded for the first thirty years of the century by Livy. Porticoes and monumental arches repeatedly figure as instruments of renovation, not only in Rome but outside it. In the year 174 B.C., while the construction of Cosa's Forum was in progress, one of the Roman censors spent part of his budget on three distant citizen colonies. Besides paving streets and digging sewers, he enclosed the Forum of one with porticoes and shops and adorned all three with monumental arches.[15]

Cosa, as an independent Latin colony, could not expect largesse of this kind from the Roman treasury, but it could build for itself in the same way. To picture what was happening in Rome and elsewhere, we must refer to Cosa's porticoes and arch (fig. 52). The former translated the continuous columnar screeen of a Hellenistic stoa into another idiom. The stocky, widely spaced columns followed the traditional proportions of Italic temple architecture. The columnar bay was not conceived as the uniform element of a screen but as a variable axial frame for something beyond it. The deep overhang of the roofs dropped the eaves to the level of the architraves, giving them that topheavy look that Vitruvius later branded illegitimate. The bold, archaic expedient of a column on the axis of a space, both as a decisive element of closure and an axial pointer, was equally foreign to Hellenistic practice. One is tempted to think of the way Roman playwrights of this epoch handled their Greek originals.

At the entrance to the fish market, the architect of the Forum had used a detached columnar bay to link one kind of space to another. To shape more significantly the moment of passage between town and Forum and to aim and channel movement from a distance, he adopted the new device of the archway. It is by far the oldest that has come down to us, but one must suppose that it was modeled on the contemporary but vanished arches in Rome. The central portal, four times the width of the narrow lateral passages, suggests the dependence of this early design on the forms of military architecture. The proportions of the central archway, a little higher than wide, approximated the basic geometrical figures of circle and square, which were and continued to be the fundamental units of Roman design.[16]

Notes

1. Coin: CF. 2232 (no. 35) in T. V. Buttrey, "Cosa: The Coins," *MAAR* 34 (1980): 16, 23, 40. Inscription: C72. 129. Concordia: G. Wissowa, *Religion und Kultus der Römer* (Munich, 1902), p. 272 f.; H. J. Rose, *Ancient Roman Religion* (London, 1948), p. 102; K. Latte, *Römische Religionsgeschichte* (Munich, 1960), p. 237 f.

2. T. Frank, "Roman Buildings of the Republic," *PAAR* 3 (1924): 39–47; G. Lugli, "Il carcere mamertino," *Capitolium* 8 (1932): 232–44. Livy, 32. 26. 17–18; cf. Livy, 26. 15. 7–8. Vitruvius, 5. 2. 1.

3. Livy, 32. 2. 7.; 33. 24. 8–9; G. Tibiletti, "La politica agraria dalla guerra annibalica ai Gracchi," *Athenaeum* n. s. 28 (1950): 192–96. Cosans in Spain: *CIL*, II, 2220, 3373, where *Cosanus/Cosana* are gentile names.

4. A Cosan family, prominent enough in the second century to have dedicated a large limestone basin on the Arx, and which might, from its singular gentile name, Tongilia, have been Etruscan, together with fragment of an Etruscan inscription on marble may suggest that Etruscan allies participated.

5. *Atrium publicum*: Polybius, 3. 26. 1; Livy, 24. 10. 9. *Atrium Libertatis*: Livy, 46. 16. 13; 45. 15. 5; Festus, 277L. *Atrium sutorium*: Varro, Ling., 6. 14; Festus, 480L. *Atria Licinia*: Cicero, *pro Quinct* 12; 25. *Atria Maenium et Titium*: Livy, 39. 44. 7. E. Welin, "Studien zur Topographie des Forum Romanun," *Acta Instituti Romani Regni Sueciae,* ser. in 8°, 6 (1963): 179–219.

6. *Forum Piscarium*: Livy, 26. 27. 3; 40. 51. 5; Varro, *Ling.* 5. 146–47; Plautus, *Curculio* 474.

7. Coins: CD. 913, CD. 916; CE. 572, CE. 859, C68. 214, C69. 223, C70. 450 (nos. 30, 34, 36, 41, 42, 54, 55) in Buttrey, "Cosa: The Coins," *MAAR* 34 (1980): 22 f., 45.

8. Roman senate: A. O'Brien Moore, "Senatus," *RE,* supplement 6 (1935): 700–719. *Curiae* of Alba Fucens and Paestum: C. Krause, "Zur baulichen Gestalt des republikanischen Comitiums," *RömMitt* 83 (1976): 31–69.

9. Pediments: Cosa, Temple of Mater Matuta: E. H. Richardson, "Sculpture Attributed to Temple D, Group B, Pedimental," *MAAR* 26 (1960): 326–28; this book, chap. IV, p. 48. Telamon, "Seven against Thebes": A. Andrén, "Architectural Terracottas from Etrusco-Italic Temples," *Acta Instituti Romani Regni Sueciae* 6 (1940): 228–34, pl. 82; O. W. von Vacano, "Ödipus zwischen den Viergespannen," *RömMitt* 68 (1961): 9–63. Luni, "Slaughter of the Niobids": Andrén, *op. cit.,* pp. 287–92, pls. 95–96; L. Banti, *Luni* (Florence, 1937), p. 49, pls. 18–22 A–P. Cività Alba, "Discovery of Ariadne": Andrén, *op. cit.,* pp. 298–300, pls. 98–100; M. Zuffa, "Il frontone e il fregio di Civitalba nel Museo Civico di Bologna," *Studi in onore di A. Caldarini e R. Paribeni* 3 (Milan, 1956), pp. 274–80. Arezzo, "Judgement of Paris(?)": Andrén, *op. cit.,* pp. 268–71, pls. 89–90. Falerii, "Rescue of Andromeda or Hesione (?)": Andrén, *op. cit.,* p. 147 f., pl. 56; Helbig, *Führer*[4], III (1969), 720, no. 2811.

10. Coin: CF. 610 (no. 35) in Buttery, "Cosa: The Coins," *MAAR* 34 (1980). Mythical sow: A. Alföldi, *Early Rome and the Latins* (Ann Arbor, 1963), pp. 19, 247, 271–78.

11. In the mid–second century B.C., the southeast end of the forum of Alba Fucens was bounded by a comparable system of square pits, revetted with slabs of stone. In its original form it consisted of a row of eleven double pits, broadside to the square. Each pit was of about the same size as those at Cosa, and each pair was separated from the next by a similar interval—ten in all. A stone lid was found beside one. It appears that the three central pairs were later replaced by single squarer pits with three others behind them, widening somewhat the four central intervals. F. De Visscher and J. Mertens, "Les puits du forum d'Alba Fucense," *BullComm* 74 (1951–52): appendice 17, 3–14; J. Mertens, *Alba Fucens I* (Brussels, 1969), pp. 92–96; cf. Krause, "Zur baulichen Gestalt des Republikanischen Comitiums," *RömMitt* 83 (1976): 45–47.

12. R. Bohn, "Die Theater–Terasse," *Altertümer von Pergamon* 4 (Berlin, 1896): 12–14, taff. IV–V; W. B. Dinsmoor, *The Architecture of Ancient Greece* (London, 1950), p. 307; M. Bieber, *The History of the Greek and Roman Theater* (Princeton, 1961), pp. 62 f., 167 f.

13. Cf. the *forma* of imperial Arausio (Orange) incised on marble slabs: A. Piganiol, "Les documents cadastraux de la colonie romaine d'Orange," *Gallia,* supplement 16 (Paris, 1962).

14. H. D. Johnson, *The Roman Tribunal* (Baltimore, 1927).

15. Livy, 41. 27. 10–13.

16. Older monumental arches in Rome: Livy, 33. 27. 3–5 (196 B.C.); 37. 3. 7 (190 B.C.). I. A. Richmond, "Commemorative Arches and City Gates," *JRS* 23 (1933): 149–74. F. E. Brown, *Roman Architecture* (New York, 1961), pp. 19–24.

IV: Arx, Port, and Forum

Soon after the Temple of Concord took its place on the Forum square and about the same time as the porticoes and archway there were receiving the finishing touches, a second temple was rising on the Arx (fig. 53). It faced the Sacred Way at the foot of its ascent to the summit, where a beaten track branched on the right toward the forecourt of the Temple of Jupiter and the postern gate. From this humbler position it looked southeastward over the wall and out to sea, turning its back on the town. The auspex on his platform above would search the heavens just over its rooftree.[1]

Unlike the Temple of Jupiter, it was a short, compact building with a perfectly square cella and a relatively shallow pronaos, about two–fifths of its depth (fig. 54). The overall length, in fact, was derived from the diagonal of the cella, and the overall height of the gable over the four columns on the facade was equal, including its finial, to the width. The walls of the cella stand on three sides up to ten feet (3.00 m.), in coursed and mortared rubblework of the kind we have noticed in the tower chambers and the Temple of Concord. The original columns, like those of the porticoes of the Forum, were of courses of sandstone slabs, shaped as segments of a circle. Walls and columns rose from a low podium of dry-laid, trapezoidal rather than polygonal, masonry, jointed to a hairsbreadth and highly finished. It was crowned by a fascia and steep torus of concrete and was reached on the facade by a flight of steps running across the intercolumniations.[2]

Centered on the facade and thirty Roman feet from it stood the broad rectangular altar. The major part of its foundation course of Vulci tufa was found in a rock-cut bedding underneath a later pavement. Its central slab covered a rough box, hewn in the rock and filled with an undisturbed deposit of dark gray ashes. These were presumably the residue of the inaugural sacrifice deposited and sealed at the temple's dedication. The bare and shelving rock that bordered the temple and its altar was not leveled or paved but was, instead, smoothed by spalling off its protruding spines and filling its deeper cracks and depressions so that the natural lines of its bed stood out as low steps and grooves. The effect was to root the temple to the ground rather than set it off from it. The color of the podium was the color of the rock from which it rose; the shapes described by the joints of its masonry were the natural rock shapes at its foot. Close to both sides of the podium a band of flaked and pitted weathering, caused by the drip from the eaves, gave the measure of the overhang of the roof.[3]

It was on these surfaces that the terracotta decoration of the superstructure fell when the roof finally gave way. Fragments of its revetments, antefixes, raking sima, and openwork cresting (fig. 55) were found along with pieces of pedimental sculpture and beam-end plaques of a cult image and of a small figured frieze. The plaques that crowned and covered the timbers above the columns displayed a richly diversified ornamentation, expressive of a transition from the older Etruscan motifs to a new set of designs that may be called Roman or Latin. Only the antefixes, sima, and cresting repeat the forms of the Temples of Jupiter and Concord. The three revetments represent the new mode. Henceforth the projecting members of temple roofs in central Italy would bear plaques molded with running loops, enclosing alternate standing and hanging palmettes, while architraves would be masked by diagonal, addorsed palmettes and spirals.[4]

As before, some of each element of the decoration had been fashioned elsewhere, this time in two workshops, probably one in or around Rome. They had been brought with their molds to Cosa, where the rest were cast by local artisans. Again, the handwrought pieces were modeled and fired at Cosa by itinerant sculptors (fig. 56). Large fragments of the pedimental figures were too few to reveal their composition or subject, but recall the style of the Temple of Concord. The scraps of the life-size cult image prove only that it was female and draped. The frieze figured a troop of dolphins and marine monsters. It might have run on the outer or inner walls of the cella or, perhaps, about the pedestal on which the cult statue stood.[5]

The occupant of our temple, facing seaward, was thus a goddess to whom ornaments evoking the sea were appropriate. In the Roman or Latin sphere these indications would point only to the ancient goddess, Mater Matuta, goddess of dawning light and childbirth, who had come to be identified with the Greek sea-goddess Leucothea, the white goddess. Her son, Melicertes or Palaemon, had, in the same way, been identified with the Roman Portunus, god of ports. Mater Matuta was worshiped, not only in Old Latium and Rome but also in the colonies, by guilds of pious women, whose members were called *matronae* (matrons) headed by *magistrae*. Other evidence of her cult at Cosa were four inscribed bases for small statues found out of context in surface levels, at least three coming from the Arx. They record the contributions of *matronae* and *magistrae* toward the sculptured offerings.[6]

The Temple of Matuta had an identical twin, slightly smaller in size. It stood on the crest of a rocky hillock, once rising sheer above the end of the lagoon of Vulci, overlooking the beach and anchorage in the lee of Cosa's promontory (figs. 6 and 57). A quarry has gouged the seaward side of the hillock, carrying with it the facade and most of the pronaos of the temple. There remain only the lowest course of the square cella, of the same build as Matuta's, together with its doorway and threshold. The temple rose straight from the rock without need of a podium. On the same, smoother surface along back and sides lay the fallen fragments of the terracotta decoration of its roof. It was the exact duplicate of the decoration of the temple on the Arx and included pedimental sculpture. The two appear to have been built and decorated together in a kinship of myth and cult that determined the identity and shape of its forms. A port calls for Portunus, the son of the sea-goddess, Mater Matuta.[7]

The temple, standing above the lagoon and the anchorage beyond the dunes, furnishes our first evidence that these were coming into use as more than a fishing beach and uncontrolled inland waterway. The relative scarcity of broken amphoras of the third and early second centuries in our excavations in and around the end of the silted lagoon and on the ancient seabed suggests that neither had borne a steady import and export traffic during the first century or more of the colony. It implies that Cosa's principal port had been Portus Herculis across the bay (fig. 3). We must assume that the Portus Cosanus, twice mentioned in connection with the second war with Carthage, was in fact the landlocked natural harbor of Hercules' Port. The temple, built around 170 B.C., must have celebrated the first harbor works of a new Portus Cosanus, whose imposing scarps and channels still look down on the summer bathers of today.[8]

A secure port off the dunes would need more protection than the promontory could afford. To stabilize the level and depth of the lagoon, fix its banks, and control excess precipitation and silting would require a permanently balanced ebb and flow to and from the sea. These requisites were realized in a major work of hydraulic engineering. The southeasternmost tip of the promontory had detached itself from the rest of the limestone mass because of some remote upheaval, leaving behind a deep and jagged cleft. It made a gigantic natural sluiceway, some 850 feet (260.00 m.) long and over 100 feet (30.00 m.) at its greatest depth (figs. 57 and 58). Its southern end met the open sea, its northern the dunes. Its width varied from 3 to 20 feet (1.00–6.00 m.), but it was nowhere impassable. To eliminate rockfalls and obtruding angles the walls, wherever necessary, were scarped perpendicular. Its bed was cleared and leveled, so as to facilitate an abundant flow of water through two tunneled openings at the seaward end (fig. 59). It debouched at its inner end into a broad, quarried recess, beyond which the face of the cliffs had been scarped vertically down 80 to 100 feet (25.00–30.00 m.), so as to form at the base a wide shelf of rock. In this was hewn the prolongation of the channel to the end of the lagoon. Through it the pulse of the tides and the push of the winds flushed the length of the lagoon and established it as a dependable waterway and fishery.[9]

The quarried masses of rock from these operations were used to enclose partially, on the seaward side, a harbor area of about 7½ acres (3 hect.) off the beach and the promontory. Starting from the cliff, the rough blocks, weighing on the average about 2½ tons, were piled on the seabed to create a continuous mole, extending east-southeastward about 360 feet (110.00 m.) and originally about 45 feet (14.00 m.) wide. Beyond the end of the mole, across the southeast, or scirocco, end of the harbor, two groups of detached breakwaters of various shapes and sizes were piled in the same way on either side of the fairway. Whereas the mole deflected the dangerous southwest seas, these breakwaters seem to have formed a sort of baffle to break the force of the scirocco seas and check sand-laden eddy currents. The dark sand of the floor on which these structures were bedded, 20 feet or so (6.00 m.) below present sea level, was archaeologically sterile. Above it lay the deposit of debris, some 2½ feet (0.75 m.) thick, that represents the activity of the harbor in ancient times.[10]

The first phase of Cosa's second port, although it was clearly a single project, consisted of two separate parts, the harbor and the lagoon. The harbor, besides its fishing fleet, would have served the town on the hill and the eastern half of its territory for import and export goods. The lagoon, besides its fisheries, would have served as the conveyer to the harbor of excess produce for export and as the distributor of imports in bulk to the region along its shores. The dunes behind the harbor both divided and linked the two, and it was there that exports and imports must have been received, handled, stored, and dispatched in areas and buildings that time and tide have erased. The colony by this time was presumably exporting dried and salt fish, wine, and perhaps grain, wool, and hides. Its imports, documented by excavation, were stone for carving, fine tablewares, glass, and Greek wines and, no doubt, many other perishable luxury goods as well.

The focus of attention now shifted to the Arx, which was being transformed by the erection of a temple that, when finished a decade or so later, would be Cosa's crowning glory. It rose on the summit, over the old high-place and sacred pit and the slopes north and east of them, supplanting and incorporating the old Temple of Jupiter (figs. 53 and 60). Behind its elevated altar court, its plan comprised three sanctuaries side by side, preceded by an exceptionally deep, half-enclosed pronaos and facade of four columns. The southwest angle of its foundations embraced the augur's platform; the sacred pit lay beneath its central axis. This ritual burial, which included the ceremonial vessels from the last sacrifice at the altar, was evidently prescribed. With it went the obligation to respect the altar and Temple of Matuta and to maintain the formal and visual alignment with the axis of the Forum, Street P, and the Sacred Way. The new temple's position, orientation, and dimensions were thus determined. As a result it faced east-northeast across the breadth of the territory, while the facade retaining wall of its forecourt was aligned with the corner of the Temple of Matuta. The temple's width, measured across the axis at the base of the walls above the foundations, was twice the distance between the center of the pit and the corner of the platform. This width, seventy Roman feet, was the basic dimension from which most of the other dimensions were derived.[11]

Since the temple could not be centered on the Sacred Way in prolongation of Street P, an artful series of adjustments was contrived in order to satisfy an ingrained and highly refined expectation of axiality. The gateway and stairs to the forecourt were shifted off the axis of the building, so as to seem to be on the axis of the Sacred Way. At the same time the facade wall of the forecourt, its gateway, and stairs, together with the stairs to the pronaos were swung imperceptibly toward the perpendicular to the approach, while the visible northeast corner was returned deceptively at a right angle. The worshiper as he stepped from Street P to the Sacred Way was met by the continuous seam that separated the two pavements and paralleled the facade ahead. To his right the retaining wall was in line with the gateway he was approaching. Beyond the retaining wall the pavement swung seemingly parallel to the north flank of the temple. To his left, as he neared the gateway, its south reveal was axial to the facade, looming beyond and, as he climbed, bringing him fully under its dominance.[12]

Apart from these refinements, the temple was designed, in all three dimensions, in terms of a rigorous and probably traditional set of proportions. The length and breadth of the whole building, including the forecourt, were as two to one, while the outside dimensions of the temple proper were four to five. Its length was divided equally between cellas and pronaos, and the latter was sectioned into closed and open halves. In breadth the three cellas were as three-, four-, and three-tenths of seventy feet. Of this dimension again the lower diameters of the columns were twentieths, their heights thirds, and the overhang of the roof a ninth.

These formulas, revealed by the building itself, are remarkably

similar to the rules set forth by Vitruvius a century and a half later
for designing an old-fashioned temple with three cellas and a tetra-
style facade. It is generally admitted, or assumed, that these rules
reflected the forms of Rome's ancient Capitolium, schematized and
handed down to Vitruvius by generations of architects. The original
Capitolium, still standing at the time of Cosa's new temple, likewise
had three cellas for Jupiter, Juno, and Minerva. Its facade of four
columns is represented on a coin struck shortly after its destruction
but before its rebuilding. Although there were other temples of similar plan to draw upon in Etruria, it is more likely that the colony
would instinctively look to the mother city for the prototype. Moreover, there are other features of the temple that seem to substantiate
the hypothesis that it was a reduced, but more or less faithful, copy
of the Capitoline temple in Rome, as it then looked.[13]

Around the base of its walls and projecting beyond the facade so
as to frame the stairs a massive podium molding covered the foundations (fig. 61). It was made up of plinth, base, die, and crown in six
courses of creamy yellow sandstone. While the plinth and die were
vertical, the base and crown were both ponderous tori of elliptical
curvature and the latter was returned inward against the wall. The
profile is rare and archaic, alien to the repertory of second-century
moldings, akin to the inturned crowns of sepulchral drums and da-
does. It is closest to the podium of the sixth-century Temple of
Casalinaccio at Ardea and related to the podium of about the same
date at Sant'Omobono at Rome. The missing podium of the Capitoline temple may well have been like it.[14]

Underneath the enclosed half of the pronaos an ample cistern
was hewn in the rock in the course of construction (fig. 62). A
source of water near at hand was, of necessity, an accessory of any
temple where animal sacrifices were continually being offered to the
gods and consumed by men. This cistern is notable both in its position within the temple and the way it was covered. Located inside
the building, it must have been filled by the rainwater that fell on the
roof. How this was caught and discharged into the cistern is indicated by elements of a compluviate catchment and an impluviate
basin. The former would have been mounted on the available supports of walls and columns so as to remain invisible from the ground

outside. The latter was sunk in the floor above the cistern (fig. 63). No other such device seems to be attested.

The rectangular cavity of the cistern was reduced in size and given semicircular ends by means of a thick lining composed of the broken roof tiles and revetments from the Temple of Jupiter. In the normal practice of Cosa the lining would have been the impost of a covering vault. Instead in this case the lining supported an elaborate stone gable, slotted at the top to receive water and pierced by two shafts to draw it. The gable is hard to justify in functional terms. Simple slab-gables had covered early cisterns in the vicinity of archaic Rome on spans of 2½ to 10 feet (0.75–3.00 m.). This type of gable, while not really comparable with Cosa's example, may point to an explanation of the complex contrivance, spanning eight feet (2.40 m.) and made up of seven different components. It is reported of Rome's Capitolium that under the pavement of its forecourt there were cisterns, known as *favisae Capitolinae*. It is likely for their time that they were covered by stone gables and it is a fair guess that they were the prototype of our anachronistic example.[15]

The terraced forecourt, too, of Cosa's Capitolium may have copied the *area Capitolina,* but the altar that stood in its midst harked back to Cosa's first altar over the sacred pit, now interred under the Cella of Jupiter. The chases, cut into the surviving slabs of the pavement for its emplacement, record its width, ten feet, and its position, centered in the forecourt but rotated 45 degrees to the facade of the temple. They also record its form which was basically a bracket shape opening out north-northeast. The orientation simulated that of the buried high-place and confronted the auspex with his familiar landmarks. A dozen battered blocks, reused nearby in the medieval castle wall, completed its shape, which echoed, with rounder base and crown, the profile of the podium (fig. 64). Among them was a fragment of one terminal pulvinus of the altar table, carved with a rosette of sixteen petals.[16]

In other respects by Cosa's standards the Capitolium was not only modern but advanced. The retaining wall of the forecourt gave an appearance much like that of Matuta's podium, but, in fact, its traditional masonry was merely the facing of a stout wall of rubble-work. The columns of the pronaos were the first at Cosa to be built of solid stone drums of gray tufa plastered as before. For the full height of the walls the local sandstone slabs were used, this, too, for the first time and to good effect (fig. 65). The south wall still stands to within an inch of its original calculated height. The stone pavement of the altar court and the gleaming white mosaic floors, bordered with black, of the three cellas surpassed the concrete floors of the earlier temples.

The intricate terracotta decoration that covered and crowned the roof timbers was now fully harmonized in the new Roman style of the second century, with one exception (fig.66). The antefixes bearing the faces of Minerva and Hercules were salvaged from the old Temple of Jupiter and remounted along the eaves with the addition of exact copies. These offsprings of Jupiter were not only appropriate but asserted the continuity of the old cult in the new. While the gables at first were without pedimental compositions, the jutting beam-ends at the sides and center were adorned with figured plaques, richly framed. Hercules again and Ganymede, cup-bearer of Jupiter, were among them (fig. 67). When the pediments were finally completed, they were of another style, the compositions more static, the figures more calmly poised, as the Romans preferred.[17]

All in all the broad, skeletal facade with its beetling roof was a powerfully sculptural force (fig. 68). The massing of its forms, spaces, and color exerted a strong attraction to the center, while the facade itself was invaded and enlivened by shifting light and shadow. The massive base and bright die were crowned, against the sky, by the airy fretwork of accent and color above. As the altar court, whose depth was the height of the facade, was filled and dominated by it, so the whole prismatic mass polarized the townscape within the walls and made itself the focus of the landscape. It was and still is a beacon, as well, to navigators far out at sea.

But the Capitolium was not merely Cosa's provincial copy of Rome's great temple. It summed up in itself and celebrated the past and present of the colony and its particular ties with Rome. It not only incorporated the remains and the cults of the old high place and the former Temple of Latin Jupiter, whose venerable image now stood in the central cella, but made room for the guardian gods of the other towns in Cosa's territory. The Jove or Tinia of Old Cosa in

the lagoon was one of these. The Argive Hercules, to whom one of
the wellheads in the pronaos was dedicated, was, no doubt, the god
of the port across the bay. In so saturate a local context, a capitolium
may seem out of place, and Cosa's Capitolium, as far as we know,
was the only one ever erected in a Latin colony. The presence of
Rome's guardian triad (Jupiter, Juno, and Minerva), with Jupiter,
Best and Greatest made one with the guardian god of a separate
state, would have been religiously and politically intolerable, had it
not implied a special bond and a special regard, the same that was
manifest when Cosa got her new recruits forty-odd years before.
Cosa's Capitolium was her thank offering to her god and Rome's for
past and present and her votive offering for their dwelling together
forever on the Arx.[18]

On the Forum, the last unoccupied area had yet to be filled. The
terrace between the Comitium and the northwest portico still awaited
a public building equal in importance to the others along that side.
The time came in the middle of the century. The building was a
basilica, the new kind of covered extension of a forum, which had
been developed in Rome over the past thirty or forty years (fig. 69).
The available terraced plot was about 120 Roman feet long, including
the back wall of the portico, and about 50 feet wide to the retaining
wall above Street 7, and measured in area about 6,000 square feet. The
specifications evidently called for an area of 10,800 square feet or
three-fourths of a square *actus*. The extra space could be obtained only
by building once again over the street on a plan proportioned as four
to three. Since the terrain sloped steeply northward, the added width
required heavy retaining walls and deep fills. At one end the plan
entailed the demolition of 2½ bays of the portico and at the other the
replacement of the adjoining wall of the Curia by a wall in line with
that of the basilica. Room was made between the substructures along
the facade for the old cistern beside the square, and it was coupled
with a second, new cistern, parallel to the old cistern and almost twice
its length.[19]

The Roman basilica was, in one sense, the offspring of the
atrium unit, in another, of the Hellenistic, two-storied portico. It
aimed on a much larger scale to provide an ample covered space,
luminous and unobstructed, for all the public uses of the open

square. In its design the technical factors of roofing and lighting were paramount. In this case, the design was, at first glance, simplicity itself (fig. 70). A broad central nave, lit by a columnar clerestory, was surrounded by an ambulatory, which, on the facade, opened to the square through a portico and at the back expanded in a windowed alcove, set off by a pair of columns. At second glance, it will be observed that the four aisles of the ambulatory were not of equal widths. The end aisles were narrowest, the rear aisle somewhat wider and the front aisle wider still. These were functional differences: greatest width toward the square for use of the outer cistern, refuge from the elements and viewing; intermediate width where the alcove, used as a tribunal, would cause congestion. It may also be noticed that the columns were not uniformly spaced, but closer on the long axis where they shouldered the load of the roof.

The lighting and roofing of the nave betrays an experimental stage in the handling of the clerestory and timber truss (fig. 71). The bases and capitals of our two orders of columns suffice to give their approximate heights. A lower drum of one of the upper columns shows that the clerestory was fully open, like the Basilica Aemilia of 179 in Rome. The height of the nave, including its blind-story and the architrave upon which the roof was seated, was some forty feet (12.20 m.) and its span fifty (15.00 m.). The raised seating discs, carved on the top of the capitals, were just sixteen inches (0.40 m.) in diameter, and the interval between trusses over fourteen feet (4.30 m.). Given the load of roof timbers and tiles, to say nothing of the wind-load, the roof might well seem a risky engineering feat. Yet it stood for some two hundred years.[20]

The basilica also reveals other advances in construction. It was the first that the walls of a permanent public building at Cosa were erected in the technique of random rubblework, akin to Roman *incertum*. Its main bearing columns were the first to be made of travertine, with Hellenistic Doric capitals and double Tuscan bases, the early Italic version of the Attic base. They were soon to be copied in the enlargement of the pronaos of the Temple of Matuta. The columns that screened the alcove had Ionic capitals, rendered in polished, violet-light-gray tufa (fig. 72). The roof of the ambulatory was flat, paved, and cantilevered over the facade, accessible through a stairwell built into the adjoining chamber of the Curia. It formed a continuous balcony around the building, providing in front a special viewing stand above the square. Such balconies, known as *maeniana*, were a feature of the basilicas on the Roman Forum.[21]

This stark building, overtopping its neighbors with pavilionlike lightness, extended, through its outer aisle, the truncated northwest portico along the adjacent side of the square (fig. 73). The two steps that raised the basilica above the pavement outside were, at the same time, prolonged the whole length of that side. They matched the steps on the opposite side, establishing a uniform base for the disparate major structures, whose uniform foil was the opposite portico. A newly minted silver piece was found on the bedding for one of the step blocks of the basilica. It had been struck in the year 157 or 156 and must have been placed there within the following decade. Finally, after a century and a quarter, the enclosure of the square was complete. The master plan of the Forum was achieved.[22]

The builders of the basilica took into account another innovation of the time. The second cistern they had included in their plan was intended to hold a substantial portion of the town's reserves of water and to free an equivalent amount for daily public use from the existing reservoir. The specific use was that of a bath building, of the kind just becoming a public amenity, and was built directly across Street O from the reservoir. Since it has not been excavated, its history remains unclear. Among its ruins a small circular room and an elevated tank above the shaft of a bucket-hoist are discernible (fig. 74). The bathing rooms were terraced on the downward side above a row of shops along Street N. There is no doubt about the water supply. The cisterns are accessible and in good repair. They were connected with the reservoir through a deep, tunnellike cistern under Street O.[23]

During the years since they had been brought under control, the twin harbors that formed the port of Cosa at the foot of the hill had evidently been thriving (fig. 75). The best evidence is the accumulation of broken terracotta containers that litter the ancient floor of the outer harbor and the areas adjacent to the end of the lagoon. Toward the end of the century a thorough renovation and improvement of both harbors was undertaken. It had probably been provoked by the collapse of parts of the towering walls of the natural sluiceway, blocking and breaching it irremediably. The urgent necessity of restoring communication between sea and lagoon would have fathered the comprehensive plan realized with uniform materials and techniques.

The abandoned natural channel from the sea was replaced by a wholly artificial one, hewn out behind the outer edge of the promontory (fig. 76). Part ditch and part tunnel, it was uniformly wider than its predecessor, but employed at its outer end a similar system of double intake tunnels. Behind these it was fitted with sluice gates for better control. At its inner end it received an auxiliary channel before it traversed the quarried recess to join the old channel into the lagoon at the foot of the scarp. In order to promote a still more active interchange of water in the end of the lagoon, a second channel was cut through the dunes about two-thirds of a mile (1 km.) to the east. The cut was revetted by rubblework retaining walls composed of tufa below water level and of limestone above. Its mouth was barred by double sluice gates.[24]

Our excavations and soundings in the extremity of the lagoon below the rocky hillside indicate that the water, circulated by these new channels, now passed to and fro through a long, narrow basin stretching from the dunes to the hillside on the north and separated from the lagoon by a dike (fig. 77). The exposed face of this was revetted with polygonal masonry of limestone, corresponding to an identical retaining wall against the slope on the opposite side, and footed on the rock or on underwater foundations of tufa rubblework. The northern end of the basin, and presumably the southern as well, was closed by a foundation wall of the same rubblework. The basin's width of 125 feet (38.00 m.) on the average was found to be divided lengthwise by similar walls into two unequal compartments, of which the wider was subdivided about in the middle. This artificially enclosed and segmented basin of shallow water, covering about 2½ acres (1 hect.) bears a strong resemblance to the ancient and medieval basins still in operation for the segregation and raising of incoming fingerlings and the trapping of outgoing mature fish in the lagoon of Orbetello and in the lagoons of the Po delta. In this case the resemblance is verified by the provision of a constant or intermittent flow of fresh water to control both the salinity and the temperature of the basin.[25]

A conduit from the lower slopes of the hillock of Portunus,

discharging into the northeast corner of the basin, must have served this purpose, which was also part of the function of an ingenious springhouse standing midway along its west bank (fig. 78). Of one build with the walls and foundations of the rest of the basin and stoutly buttressed against the pitch of the shelving rock it stood on, its central unit was a collecting chamber, filled by the numerous outlets of a welling spring. The overflow fed an open tank in front and spilled in a trough across a buttressing platform into the inner compartment of the basin. The principal function of the little building, however, was to support the mechanism of a wooden bucket-conveyer, installed above the collecting chamber. This was designed to raise the water and to discharge it into an aqueduct, which carried it on piers across the basin and along the dike to the emporium on the dunes. There it would have served the multifarious uses of the busy commercial center besides providing drinking water for the ships in the harbor.[26]

The overall plan of renovation also included the improvement of the outer harbor. The mole that fended the southwestern seas was now made useful as a wharf, connected with the dunes. With the mole as foundation a staggered row of four or five massive piers, rising above water level, was erected. At an angle from the mole a row of four or five more reached the dunes. The remains of two on the mole and three on the inward leg are still extant. Like the foundations in the basin, they were laid underwater in coffer dams and were constructed of tufa rubblework. Limestone was used above the waterline. Besides breaking the swells across the mole, the piers, joined by a masonry or timber superstructure, would have permitted vessels to lie alongside, discharging and loading their cargoes. The complex of harbors and fishery, skillfully adopted to the natural features of promontory, dunes, and lagoon, was another expression of Cosa's maturity. The fragments of the containers that document Cosa's commerce and that remain immured in the masonry of all these installations bring us to the beginning of the next century.

Notes

1. Vide chap. III, p. 25; chap. II, pp. 16, 17; F. E. Brown, "Cosa II: The Temples of the Arx," *MAAR* 26 (1960): 25.

2. Brown, "Cosa II: The Temples of the Arx," *MAAR* 26 (1960): 25–32.

3. Ibid., pp. 32–34.

4. L. Richardson, Jr., "Cosa II: The Temples of the Arx," *MAAR* 26 (1960): 182–98.

5. E. H. Richardson, "Sculpture Attributed to Temple D, Group B, Pedimental," *MAAR* 26 (1960): 324–30.

6. Lucretius, 5. 656; Cicero, *Tusc.* 1. 28; *Nat. D.* 3. 48; Ovid, *Fasti* 6. 543–47. Cf. G. Wissowa, *Religion und Kultus der Römer* (Munich, 1902), pp. 97–99; G. F. Maule and H. R. W. Smith, "Votive Religion at Caere," *CPCA* 4, no. 1 (1959): 74–87; G. Radke, *Die Götter Altitaliens* (Münster, 1965), pp. 206–9. R. Bloch, "Recherches sur les religions de l'Italie antique," *Centre de recherches d'histoire et de philologie, Ecole pratiques des Hautes Etudes,* III, 7 (1976): 1–9. *Matronae* and *Magistrae:* at Cosa, *CIL,* XI, 2630=I², 1994, CB 580/493 and CE 108; at Pisaurum, *CIL,* I, 176, 177=I², 372, 379; at Cales, *CIL,* X, 4650, 4660; at Cora, *CIL,* X, 6511; at Praeneste, *CIL,* XIV, 2997, 3006.

7. See articles by F. E. Brown, E. H. Richardson, and L. Richardson in *MAAR* 26 (1960): 143–45, 204 f., 330–32.

8. *Portus Cosanus* =Portus Herculis: Livy, 22. 11. 6; 30. 39. 1.

9. F. E. Brown, "Cosa I: History and Topography," *MAAR* 20 (1951): 92 f.; E. Rodenwalt and H. Lehmann, "Die antike Emissare von Cosa Ansedonia," *SBHeidel,* math.-natur. Kl. (1962): 3–31.

10. A. M. McCann and J. D. Lewis, "The Ancient Port of Cosa," *Archaeology* 23 (1970): 201–11; G. Schmiedt, *Il livello antico del mar Tirreno* (Florence, 1972), pp. 25–30.

11. Brown, "Cosa II: The Temples of the Arx," *MAAR* 26 (1960): 49 f.

12. Ibid., p. 102.

13. Ibid., pp. 90–93. Vitruvius 4. 7. 1–5. Coin: Moneyer M. Volteius M. f., 78 B.C.; M. H. Crawford, *Roman Republican Coinage* (Cambridge, 1974), vol. 1, no. 385/1, p. 399 f.; vol. 2, pl. XLIX.

14. Brown, "Cosa II: The Temples of the Arx," *MAAR* 26 (1960): 69–73. L. T. Shoe, "Etruscan and Republican Roman Mouldings," *MAAR* 28 (1965): 39–45, pls. I–III; 84–88, pl. XXIII; E. Gjerstad, "Early Rome III," *Acta Instituti Romani Regni Sueciae* ser. in 4°, 17:3 (1960): 382, fig. 245.

15. Brown, "Cosa II: The Temples of the Arx," *MAAR* 26 (1960): 59–65, 103, 108; T. Ashby, "Il castello d'acqua arcaica del Tuscolo," *Bull. Comm.* 57 (1929): 161–82; L. and S. Quilici, *Antemnae* (Consiglio Nazionale delle ricerche, Roma, 1978), pp. 35–36.

16. Brown, "Cosa II: The Temples of the Arx," *MAAR* 26 (1960): 81–84; Shoe, "Etruscan and Republican Roman Mouldings," *MAAR* 28 (1965): 981 pl. XXVI, 2; cf. M. Torelli, "Terza campagna di scavo a punta della vipera (S. Marinella)," *StEtr* 35 (1968): 332, fig. 3.

17. L. Richardson, "Cosa II: The Temples of the Arx," *MAAR* 26 (1960): 206–31; E. H. Richardson, "Sculpture Attributed to the Capitolium," *MAAR* 26 (1960): 332–69.

18. E. H. Richardson, "Sculpture Attributed to Temple D, Group B, Pedimental," *MAAR* 26 (1960): 369–72. *Diovis* of Orbetello: R. de Witt, "Scavi di

Orbetello (Cosa)," *BdI* (1858): 103–5. Hercules Argivus: CB 679/680, CB 482/CC 877.

19. Old cistern: vide chap. II, p. 22; chap. III, p. 39.

20. Basilica Aemilia: Livy, 40. 51. 5. Excavations: G. Carettoni, "Esplorazioni nella basilica Emilia," *NSc* 73 (1948): 111–28. Coin representation: moneyer M. Aemilius Lepidus 61 B.C.; Crawford, *Roman Republican Coinage* (Cambridge, 1974), vol. 1, no. 419/3a, p. 441; vol. 2, pl. LII.

21. Maeniana: Cicero, *Acad.* pr. 2. 22. 70; Vitruvius, 5. 1. 2; Festus, 120L; L. Lehmann Hartleben, "Maenianum and Basilica," *AJP* 59 (1938): 280–96.

22. Coin: CD. 1050 (no. 67) in T. V. Buttrey, "Cosa: the Coins," *MAAR* 34 (1980): 23. Cf. Crawford, *Roman Republican Coinage*(Cambridge, 1974), vol. 1, no. 197/la; vol. 2, pl. XXXI.

23. Brown, "Cosa I: History and Topography," *MAAR* 20 (1951): 82–84; cf. Vitruvius, 5. 10.

24. Brown, "Cosa I: History and Topography," *MAAR* 20 (1951): 93–96; McCann and Lewis, "The Ancient Port of Cosa," *Archaeology* 23 (1970): 201–11.

25. A. M. McCann, "Excavations at the Roman Port of Cosa," *AJA* 77 (1973): 220 (abstract). Cf. R. Del Rosso, *Pesche e peschiere antiche e moderne* (Grosseto, 1933), p. 52 f.

26. McCann, "Excavations at the Roman Port of Cosa," *AJA* 77 (1973): 220.

V: Town and Country

Having lingered, perhaps immoderately, over the public aspects of Cosa's development, it is time to turn to what we have learned about its private life. The public buildings and public works of a city-state such as Cosa were the most conspicuous and most durable components of the urban environment they shaped. They represented and characterized the tendencies of one urban community in comparison with others in the historical context of its era and culture. The private buildings were less prominent in the townscape and also less permanent. As they were more variably responsive to the tastes and the fortunes of their owners, they reflected the degrees of individuality of the members of the community. Our notion of the domestic architecture of the town must be drawn from a very limited sample of excavated dwellings. Eight in all with adjoining parts of four others, they were situated in two adjacent blocks, skirted by Street 5, near the center (fig. 79). There is reason to think, nevertheless, that they were typical for the most part. The visible remains of eighty-five or ninety other structures, presumably houses, lie scattered over the site.

It has been assumed from the outset that the house plots of the first colonists were, along with the streets and public places, laid out on the bare rock and subsoil of the site. It has also been noted that none of the houses we have unearthed was erected before the third quarter of the third century.[1] This is to say that at least a generation and more of Cosans made shift to dwell on their plots in temporary quarters, of which no trace has been found. This state of affairs was accounted for by hard times and more urgent priorities. The lack of vestiges is understandable from the nature of the site. The great majority of house plots lay on the northern slopes below the Arx, the eastern height and the Forum saddle. This kind of terrain did not provide the relatively level surfaces that ancient builders and house-holders favored. A proper horizontal house had either to be raised on a terrace or seated on a rock-hewn shelf. In either case the terrace would bury or the shelf destroy any remains of previous habitation.

The original house plots, as delimited by the houses eventually built on them, were narrow strips running across the width of each block from street to street and oriented southeast-northwest. Each of these was evidently to be divided about equally between a dwelling and a garden. For reasons of light, temperature, and hygiene, the dwelling normally occupied the upper southeastern half of the plot. There it received the maximum of sunlight and, by the same token, of warmth in winter and coolness in summer, as well as natural drainage toward the garden below. Accordingly, the upper half was terraced by a median retaining wall to the height of the upper street, while the garden was roughly cut down to the level of the lower street. These massive retaining walls, laid up with unshaped blocks of limestone and exposed by the erosion of the site, can be seen stretching along the middle of many of the unexcavated blocks. They signal the general ubiquity of the design and practice that our few excavated plots reveal.

Beneath the terrace and within the foundation of each dwelling lay its cistern for the storage of the rainwater collected from the roofs (fig. 80) and its cesspool for the household sewage. Both were hewn in the sloping rock before the terrace was leveled up: the cistern toward the front of the house, the cesspool toward the back. The one was made watertight by a lining of cement while the other used the fissured rock for the disposal of its wastes. Two of our oldest houses retained, throughout their lifetimes, their original plans. The original plans of two others, although modified at various times, were still legible (fig. 81).

On their plots, twice as long as wide, all four had been built to the same basic plan, of which the principal elements were fixed and the others adaptable, within limits, to circumstances and personal convenience. A vestibule corridor, flanked by a room at either side, led in from the street to an inner court set across the full width of the house and above the cistern. Behind it were two rooms, side by side.

On the left a squarish room, wide open to the court, trapped the winter sun. The room on the right was no fixed size or shape and connected either from the court or from the left-hand room with the rearmost division of the house. This was a narrow, transverse space above the cesspool, variously divided across its width into kitchen, bath, and store-closet, and gave access to the garden. The plan provided a compact house for a single family with an open area, a living-dining room, cooking and bathing facilities, and two or three bedrooms, as well as a garden for pleasure and profit. A bedroom might be added, or the space used as a stable for the family donkey, a little portico might shade part of the court, the kitchen or bathroom might expand into the adjacent room, but the fixed functions and spaces remained immutable.

The better preserved parts of our four examples show that they were constructed of the same materials as the buildings around the three sides of the Forum square (fig. 82). Above their terraces low socles of squared limestone blocks carried walls of sun-dried bricks. Their inner courts were designed for light, not for the purpose of collecting water (fig. 83). The rainfall on their roofs was brought from the eaves to the ground by means both of water spouts over the doorways (fig. 84), discharging into catch basins below, and of vertical pipes built into the reveals of the doorways. Thence, in either case, it was conveyed in covered conduits to the cisterns. Conduits from both ends of one house have survived. This, taken together with the deliberate separation between the front and back parts of each house on either side of the court, seems to imply that each house was covered by lean-to roofs, pitching forward and backward from the open space between.

Within the excavated area nine houses of this type, aligned along Streets M and N, had originally been built singly or in pairs, with party walls. Eleven others would have filled the two blocks. The walls emerging from the unexcavated house blocks over the rest of the site are generally at intervals conforming to the lateral and longitudinal dimensions of the same kind of plan. This evidence may be accepted as indicating that at one time all or most of the houses in the town were more or less alike. The basic plan, so neatly and uniformly articulated, so simply and unconventionally roofed and so unlike the Roman atrium—or the Hellenistic peristyle house—has no counterpart, to my knowledge, in contemporary Italy or elsewhere. Since the room open on the court resembled a *tablinum,* one might surmise that the plan had been derived from a Roman or Latin proto- type, of which no other examples have come to light. Even so the unified design and its application to the town plan smacks of eco- nomical housing for an egalitarian community, in short, colonial housing.[2]

Be that as it may, this apparently somewhat utopian scheme soon yielded to the facts of life. The inevitable impoverishment of some citizens and enrichment of others and the extinction and prolif- eration of families caused some houses and garden plots to be modi- fied and some to change hands in the second century, probably in conjunction with the arrival of the new colonists. This, no doubt, aggravated the lack of available building space within the tightly drawn circuit of the walls. About this time, the owners of two of our houses gave up their gardens so that new homes could be built (fig. 85). These converted plots were apparently used by members of their growing families, since both new houses communicated with the old by means of the incorporated stairs which had formerly led to the gardens. The new houses, built on the lower half of the original plots, faced northwestward on the lower street. The reversed orien- tation called for radical rearrangements of the prevailing house plan in order that the essential open room face south on the court.

A generation or so later two other houses, side by side in the next block, made room for needed living space by sacrificing a part of their gardens (fig. 86). The owners of each house moved its kitchen, bath, and storeroom into an extension at the back over a new cesspool and converted the former facilities to other uses. One of the additions was a cellar at the level of the garden, reached by two flights of stairs and covered by a roof or deck. The other was terraced up to the original level above and roofed like the rest of the house. Its disused cesspool was found to contain the last broken crockery that had been dumped into it, all from about the middle of the century.

The process of social and economic differentiation is exem- plified, within the excavated zone, by two houses of the decades before and after the turn of the second and first centuries. The earlier represents the acquisition of two of the original houses and their drastic remodeling for the purposes of a prosperous supplier of commodities to the Roman government (fig. 87). Little but the shell of the old buildings was kept and the new plan was strikingly idiosyncratic. It divides into three functional units. One may be called the representational unit, consisting of an imposing entry from the street, an outer courtyard opening to a capacious exedra, flanked by a closed, more intimate reception room. The doorway was recessed and fitted with benches. Beside the inner vestibule was the gatekeeper's lodge. A wide doorway from the courtyard admitted to the domestic unit, comprising an inner courtyard with the cistern wellhead, a kitchen, pantry, and bath. The third unit was composed of a large covered space with its own doorway on the street—probably a stable or warehouse—and, behind it, another spacious courtyard. The owner had left behind him the discarded shards of two fine black-glaze vessels on which he had self-consciously scratched his name, Quintus Fulvius.[3]

He had also left behind him, buried under the pantry floor, a bulging, narrow-necked jar crammed to the brim with silver coins (fig. 88). The two thousand-odd *denarii* he had accumulated as capital and tucked away fall into two parts. A fifth to a quarter was made up of circulated pieces covering a century from the earliest issues of the *denarius* down to the years 110 to 105 B.C. From then on the remaining four-fifths to three-fourths consisted of relatively large amounts of annually added issues down to 72–71 B.C., when the jar could hold no more. These coins for the most part were in mint condition and must have been paid directly from the Roman Treasury. This singular distribution suggests that our rising businessman, having secured a government contract sometime in the last decade of the second century, bought the two old houses and rebuilt them to his requirements, while, with the remainder of his savings, he began the new accumulation from his profits. The queer third unit of the house seems designed for the handling and storage of something bulky, such as grain, timber, or draft animals, any of which were in constant demand by the state.[4]

The second and later of our two houses was the most stately of

our sample (figs. 89 and 90). It occupied five of the gardens of the
upper block; two were full-length and three had been previously
curtailed by their former owners. On this extended and irregular
terrain, sloping down to Street 5, the new house with its garden was
freely designed lengthwise of the block. Garden and house were
terraced one above the other and separated by a breast-high retaining
wall. The ground floor of the house, raised above the streets on two
sides and cut out of the rocky slope on the other, was organized
around a square court with a sunken catch basin. Two of its adjoining sides were dominated by capacious halls wide open to the court
on the southeast and northeast. These halls were exedrae, winter and
summer reception rooms, one sunny, the other shadowed. On one
of the opposite sides the vestibule from Street 5 opened alongside an
elegantly paved chamber with an alcove dais for the bed. On the
other were two cool, rock-walled storerooms for comestibles. The
four corner spaces were filled—clockwise—by a kitchen and bath
beside the vestibule, an ample family room and a closet, a dining
room and a hidden storage chamber, accessible only from the stairwell to an upper story. At the back of the house a broad and lofty
portico of three columns gave onto the garden, which was reached
by a flight of four steep steps.

While the forms of an atrium house were not in evidence, a sort
of localized symmetry and axiality pervaded the central area. The
court was not centered in the house, nor the basin within the square
of the court. It was, however, centered in the square of the eaves of
the court, which overhung more on two sides than on the others.
Not the basin but the wellhead at its corner stood on the axes of the
two open halls and formed a reassuring point of stability in a flowing
context. House and garden were, in fact, designed as one along an
oblique visual axis running from the doorway on Street 5, across the
basin in the court, through a doorway at the back of the summer
reception room and a bay of the portico, to the west corner of the
garden (fig. 91). The garden was glimpsed from the moment of
entering and gradually revealed as one penetrated to the portico. It
was part of the dining room, seen through a picture doorway at eye
level from the couches. The garden itself, as it sloped from the foot
of the portico up to a parapet with a central opening, had its own

local symmetry. At the bottom, beside the top of the steps from the house, a rustic, rock-cut pool caught the drip from the roof of the portico. From either end of the portico two paths converged on the opening in the upper parapet and on a tree beyond it, one of several that shaded and closed the vista. In the transverse area behind the parapet, shrubbery lined a crosswise path that led from a wicket gate on the street side to a raised pergola on the other.

The walls of the principal rooms of the mansion were decorated with parti-colored plaster in the late Hellenistic masonry style. Their floors were paved with reddish or gray concrete inset with tesselated patterns and borders of white or black. A sounding under one of them yielded a newly minted bronze coin, struck in 91 or 85 B.C., and it is safe to say that the house was erected during the second decade of the first century. Its inventive and relatively sophisticated design was a far cry from the tenaciously repeated forms of the older dwellings and seems to flout the look of equality to which they had so long adhered. It has the air of a frankly superior person in his provincial community, who openly asserted his individuality as well as his station.[5]

Our sample of the domestic architecture of the town makes evident the tendency, in the latter years of the colony, toward a more pronounced hierarchy of wealth and prestige in the Roman pattern. It is not surprising to find the same trend in the country side. Our broad survey of farm sites over the whole *ager cosanus* permits a rough estimation of the farms that were under cultivation around the turn of the first century B.C. (fig. 92). Of these the smallest and poorest, measured by the amount and quality of their remains and by their proximity to others, may be assumed to represent the original freeholds handed down from the founding. Many are within 300 yards (275 m.) of one another. They account for about 60 percent of the total. A second category of sites, marked by terracing, more solid construction and flooring, decorative features and wider spreads of debris, constitutes about 25 percent of the whole. They may be taken to represent the result of the normal process of the accumulation of property in fewer hands by purchase, foreclosure, marriage, or inheritance. Finally, some 15 percent of the sample consists of monumental country houses on relatively large estates in the choicest of locations.[6]

The three best preserved of such villas, lying within a radius of 2½ miles (4 km.) of the town, and hence suburban, shared similar sites and architectural features (figs. 93 and 94). They crowned eminences, in view of and overlooking their fields, not necessarily bound by the grid lines of the land. Each manor house, apart from its outbuildings, stood on a platform supported by stepped terraces (fig. 95). Embanked or structural within their retaining walls, these contained vaulted arcades, cisterns, storerooms, corridors, and stairways. Their singular most common feature was the buttressing of the lowest retaining wall by miniature cylindrical turrets, embellished above the top of the wall with two ranges of arched niches (fig. 96). The outer enclosure of each manor house was thus, in appearance, a toy fortification. The niches, one must imagine, were filled in their seasons with flower pots or nesting songbirds, and the sham wall was a quaintly emblematic conceit of the urbanity or the seclusion within.

One of the upper platforms has recently been partially explored by soundings and another is in process of excavation. The results have given the excavators the preliminary impression from the finds of coins and pottery that both houses were erected during the first quarter of the first century B.C. The results so far also seem to indicate that the central spaces of both had originally been planned in the axial sequence of atrium, peristyle, and colonnaded balconies. This was the plan prescribed for suburban villas by Vitruvius and is illustrated by the examples of the first century in Campania, near Pompeii, Herculaneum, Stabia, and now Oplontis. Our turreted walls, too, will recall the literary tradition of turreted villas in Campania, from Scipio Africanus down to Julius Caesar. It is not improbable that turrets and plans alike were imported to Cosa's countryside by the same Campanian architect.[7]

However that may be, it seems clear that by the early first century the distribution of land in the territory ran parallel with that in the town. The picture we have been able to draw from our sampling there shows us old, almost unchanged houses on their original plots cheek by jowl with new, renovated and enlarged houses and latterly with mansions, two or three times as big. The picture of the countryside is its counterpart. The recent large estates, even though each may have absorbed between seventy and ninety original free-holds, could not, in any sense, be described as domains, *latifundia,* of the kind ancient writers were fond of lamenting and the numerous agrarian laws sought to check—thousands of acres tilled by thousands of slaves. The largest of our three roughly measurable estates, surrounded as they were by the contemporary subsistence plots and middle-sized farms, could have encompassed no more than 400 acres (160 hect.). Evidently it was not the *ager cosanus* that dismayed Tiberius Gracchus by its spectacle of desolation as he passed along the Via Aurelia on his way to Spain in 137. Nor was it in the ports of Cosa that the astute old soldier, Marius, chose to land on his return from Africa in 87, but at Etruscan Telamon, beyond the northern border of the colony. It was there, in the territory of Heba, that he found the slaves and dispossessed freemen—perhaps his veterans—to fill his forty ships.[8]

The wealth that built the more prosperous farms of Cosa came, no doubt, from cereals, livestock and its products, oil, and wine. Only the latter, by their instruments of production and handling, provide positive information. The remains of a sizable farm, by a spring only 550 yards (500 m.) from the northwest gate of the town, include a well-preserved pressingroom (fig. 97) in addition to scattered walls, cisterns, and tanks. It was neatly floored with brick and fitted, like Cato's, with the stone supports of four beam-presses, obviously for wholesale production. Then again our excavations in the town and around the port have yielded thousands of fragments of wine containers and a few whole amphoras (fig. 98). The vast majority, of a size to bear witness, had neither been coated with pitch on the inside for shipment nor faceted by rubbing against the neighboring amphoras in the hold of a ship. This signifies that such amphoras were made locally and were handy for other uses or had been broken before they could be pitched and filled. One of the uses, at Cosa, as elsewhere, was adding bulk to fills.

Over 800 fragmentary or whole amphoras, of all periods, bore impressed stamps, presumably to identify their manufacturers. About 10 percent of these, by far the greatest number found in any one place on land, were the stamps of a certain Sestius, abbreviated SES, SEST, or SESTI and accompanied by a number of symbols whose meaning remains unsolved. The amphoras of Sestius have been found in wrecks all along the coasts of the western Mediterranean. Seventeen hundred of them were found in the famous wrecks off the Grande Congloué near Marseilles. They turn up in many places far inland in south and western Europe and less frequently east of Italy. Sestius did a brisk business either in empty containers or filled with his own vintages. His reliably datable stamps, found at Cosa or elsewhere, were all in contexts of the late second to early first centuries B.C.—none earlier, although Roman amphoras had been labeled before.[9]

We should expect, from the pristine condition of many of Sestius's amphoras found at Cosa, that he or his family lived or owned property in the territory of Cosa around this time. It happens that the best known of the few recorded Sestii fills the bill. The Roman knight, Publius Sestius—son of Lucius, Quaestor in 63, Tribune of the Plebs in 57, Praetor in 54 or 50, and Proconsul 49 to 47, bosom friend of Cicero, who defended him in court with one of his most eloquent pleadings—had an estate at Cosa. He was also familiar with the Roman West. We know of at least two occasions on which he visited Marseilles and Gaul. Moreover his son, Lucius Sestius Quirinalis, Consul in 23, was one of the first of the long line of Roman aristocrats who owned tile factories. There is no likelier manufacturer of the slim but sturdy amphoras that bore their family name than Publius or, perhaps, his father. One or another of the larger estates near the town would have been theirs, and we have reason to hope that the current interest in Cosa's countryside may reveal which it was.[10]

In 90 B.C., Cosa, along with all the other Latin colonies, had unexpectedly acquired Roman citizenship by virtue of the Julian law. This wartime enactment aimed to pacify and divide Rome's rebellious allies and to confirm and reward the staunch allegiance of the Latins. In effect it merged their old citizenship and institutions with those of the self-governing Roman municipalities around them, each a commonwealth in the greater *res publica* of all Roman citizens. Cosa's territory was not involved in the bitter fighting, and the change of status is not detectable in the ruins and rubbish of the town. Although the Roman tribe to which Cosa was assigned remains unknown, inscriptions show that the junior magistrates of the new municipality continued to be titled *quaestors* and *aediles*. The citizenship seems to have made it easier for Romans of Cosa to emigrate to the metropolis and for Romans from elsewhere to amass their properties in the *ager cosanus*. The prominent Cosan family, the Tongilii, perhaps of Etruscan extraction, apparently moved about this time to Rome, where one of them enjoyed the favors of Catiline and where their slaves and freedmen later on were buried with those of the imperial house. It was likely after 90 that Nero's ancestors, the Domitii Ahenobarbi, and perhaps Vespasian's grandmother, acquired their Cosan estates.[11]

In any case Cosa's colonial mission had reached its end. The colony had performed its task. It had guarded the frontier. It had built a nucleus of Latinity in the midst of the Etruscans. It had grown and prospered to become a sound and serviceable unit of the Roman Commonwealth. What could not have been foreseen was that Cosa itself, within a generation, would suffer a much more drastic change. It would cease, for a time, to exist and would never again be what it had been. Excavation has shown that all the houses we have uncovered, together with the shops and atrium buildings around three sides of the Forum square had been burnt out and left in ruins. One Cosan lost his life in the cistern of our latest and largest house (fig. 99). His skeleton fails to tell us whether he was thrust in or had lowered himself in an effort to escape. The catastrophe obviously occurred after the burial of the hoard of coins in the nearby double house in 71–70 B.C. The discarded pottery and lamps, accumulated in the cesspools after their last cleaning suit a date within the ensuing decade.

The conflagration was accompanied or immediately followed by rough-and-ready modifications of the town walls. One of the square towers flanking the northeast gate was replaced by a round tower of coarse masonry, filled with earth and amphoras of the early first century. The east and south extremities of the wall were turned into forts. Around the eastern height makeshift rooms and a cistern were installed behind the curtains. The south angle beside the Capitolium became a sort of bastion raised on an embankment, filled with earth, ashes, the rubble of walls of masonry and sun-dried bricks, and, again, layers of amphoras. It covered, impiously, the lower three courses of the temple podium. The latest of the coins dropped into this chaotic fill was a fairly fresh, plated *denarius,* struck in 85 B.C. The latest pottery was the same as that from the houses.

The denuded aspect of most of the peripheral areas of the site indicates that the conflagration was far more widespread than what has been brought to light. The temples and major public buildings of the Arx and the center that were spared give clear signs of a total abandonment, which, it can be estimated, lasted some forty years. These closely and sequentially related archaeological data are best interpreted more or less as follows. During the decade 70 to 60 B.C. unknown persons deliberately sacked and destroyed most of the town, driving out, killing, or enslaving the populace. They then hastily fortified chosen strongpoints on the circuit of the walls and presently departed without leaving a trace. This scenario suggests a ferocious raid with the intent to establish a base for further operations, which were prematurely checked.

If this hypothetical series of events is not entirely fortuitous and isolated, it ought to be related to some known, historical situation of the time. The only one that appears to satisfy the conditions is that of the piratical inroads along the Tyrrhenian coast which were suppressed by Pompey's admiral, Lucius Gellius, in 67. The wave of organized piracy on an enormous scale, moving westward from the Aegean, reached Italian waters as early as 75. In the intervening years the fleets of ever-bolder buccaneers had carried off Roman magistrates and noble Roman dames for ransom, destroyed a Roman fleet in the harbor of Ostia, and seized and sacked easily defensible headlands like the Lacinian promontory, Misenum, and Gaeta, as bases for inland forays. Cosa was just such another and not the only one in Etruria. Her neighbor, Telamon, was probably destroyed as well. In Pompey's grand and successful design for eliminating piracy from the Mediterranean in forty days Gellius's command was specifically the Tuscan shore.[12]

Cosa had passed unscathed through the turmoil of the eighties in Etruria only to be struck down by an outrageous and irrelevant reversal of fortune, a true peripeteia. What was left of the town which the colonists had built was destined eventually to be patched up, but it was never remade. Its future occupants were not to increase but to dwindle, leaving it at last to the archaeologists as the most perfect example of a Roman town in the making during the third and second centuries B.C. Cosa's real and enduring significance under the principate was that it had been one of the thirty Latin colonies, the originals on which the legal concept of Latin rights, *ius Latii,* was modeled. Made available to hundreds of peoples and towns, remote in time and place from Latium or Latins, it served as their stepping stone to full citizenship, until all within the confines of the empire were Romans.[13]

Notes

1. Vide chap. I, p. 8; chap. II, p. 25.

2. F. E. Brown, "Scavi a Cosa-Ansedonia (1965–1966)," *BdA* 52 (1967): 37–41. Cf. a recent survey of sevety-five Greek and Roman houses: J. W. Graham, "Origins and Interrelations of the Greek and the Roman House," *Phoenix* 20 (1966): 3–31.

3. Q. FVL(vi): C66.220, base of a bowl; C66.855, fragment of a pyxis.

4. Brown, "Scavi a Cosa-Ansedonia (1965–1966)," *BdA* 52 (1967): 40; M. H. Crawford, *Roman Republican Coin Hoards* (London, 1969), table XIII, p. 105; T. V. Buttrey, "Cosa: The Coins," *MAAR* 34 (1980): 74–76.

5. V. Bruno, "A Town House at Cosa," *Archaeology* 23 (1970): 233–41. Coin: C70.448 (no. 91) in T. V. Buttrey, "Cosa: The Coins," *MAAR* 34 (1980): 24. Cf. M. H. Crawford, *Roman Republican Coinage* (Cambridge, 1974), vol. 1, nos. 339/4 and 350B/3, pp. 340, 366; vol. 2, pl. XLVI.

6. S. L. Dyson, "Settlement Patterns in the Ager Cosanus," *NSc* (forthcoming): 14–18.

7. L. Quilici and S. Quilici Gigli, "Ville dell'agro cosano con fronte a torrette," *RivIstArch* 23 (1976): 11–64. Turretted villas: Seneca, *Ep.* 5. 51. 11; 8–13. 86. 4; cf. J. H. D'Arms, *Romans on the Bay of Naples* (Cambridge, Mass., 1970), pp. 1–38; O. Elia, *Pitture di Stabia* (Naples, 1957), p. 52, tavv. XXV, XXVI.

8. Plutarch, *Gracchi* 8, 9; *Marius* 41, 3–5. Cf. W. V. Harris, *Rome in Etruria and Umbria* (London, 1971), pp. 202–8; D. B. Nagle, "The Etruscan Journey of Tiberius Gracchus," *Historia* 25 (1976): 487–89.

9. E. L. Will, "Les amphores de Sestius," *RAE* 7 (1956): 224–44; F. Benoit, "L'epave du Grand Congloué a Marseille," *Gallia,* supplément 14 (1961): 42–70; W. Culican and J. E. Curtis, "The Punic Wreck in Sicily. Pt. 2: The Pottery from the Ship," *International Journal of Nautical Archaeology* 3 (1974): 44–47; E. L. Will, "New Light on the Sestius Question," *AJA* 79 (1975): 151 (abstract).

10. F. Münzer, "P. Sestius," *RE* 2A (1923): 1886–90; T. R. S. Broughton, *The Magistrates of the Roman Republic* (New York, 1962), vol. 2, pp. 168, 176, 202, 264, 278; Cicero, *pro Sestio* 3. 7, 33. 71; *ad Att.* 15. 27. 1.

11. *Lex Julia de civitate:* G. Rotondi, *Leges publicae populi Romani* (ed. Hilde-

sheim 1962) 338 f.; cf. A. N. Sherwin-White, *The Roman Citizenship*[2] (Oxford, 1973), pp. 147–52. *Quaestors and aediles:* inscriptions CG.247, CA. 140/CC. 266. *Tongili:* vide chap. III, p. 45, n. 4; Cicero, *in Catilinam* 2. 2. 4; *CIL,* VI, indices, fasc. V, p. 5678. *Domitii Ahenobarbi:* Cicero, *ad Att.* 9. 6. 2, 9. 9. 3; Caesar, *Bellum Civile* 1. 34. 2. *Tertulla:* Suetonius, *Vesp.* 2. 1.

12. Plutarch, *Pompey* 24–29; Appian, *Mithradat.* 92–95, Cassius Dio, 36. 20–37. Cf. Cicero, *Leg. Man.* 32; Sallust, *Hist.* (Maurenbracher) I. 47. 7. H. A. Ormerod, *Piracy in the Ancient World* (Liverpool, 1924), pp. 227–41. Telamon: G. F. Gamurrini, *NSc* (1888): 682–91; G. Caputo, "Telamon," *EAA* VII (1966): 583 f. W. V. Harris, *Rome in Etruria and Umbria* (London, 1971), pp. 206 f., 258.

13. A. Bernardi, *Nomen Latinum* ("Studia Ghisleriana" 1973), pp. 118–33; A. N. Sherwin-White, *The Roman Citizenship*[2] (Oxford, 1973), pp. 114–16, 279–87, 360–79.

Plates

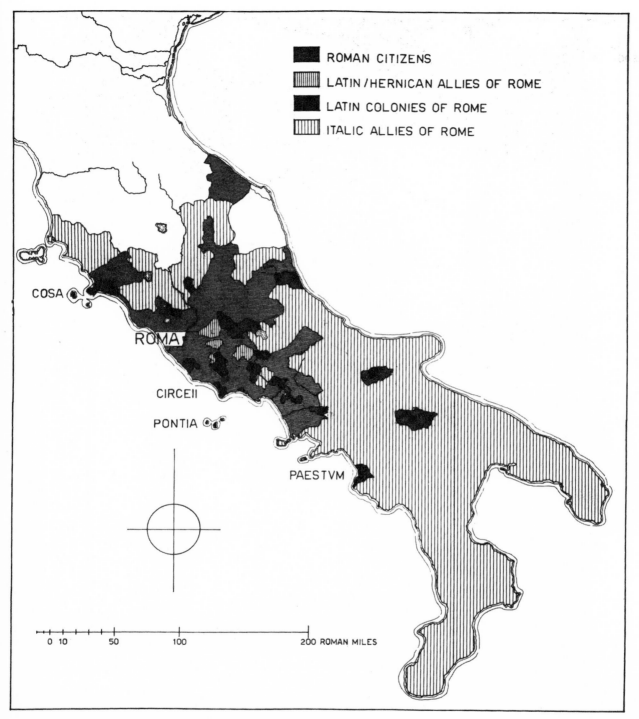

COSA

ROMA

CIRCEII

PONTIA

PAESTVM

0 10   50   100   200 ROMAN MILES

Fig. 1. The Roman Commonwealth in 270 B.C.

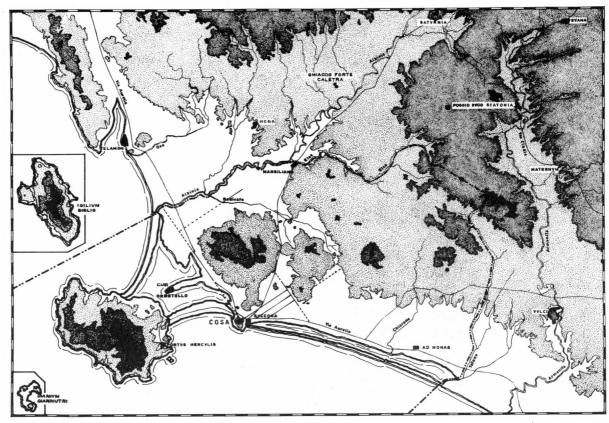

Fig. 2. The Colony of Cosa and surroundings.

Fig. 3. Mount Argentario and Portus Herculis.

Fig. 4. Coastal plain, east of Cosa.

Fig. 5. Lagoon of Orbetello, west of Cosa.

Fig. 6. Lagoon of Vulci, east of Cosa.

Fig. 7. Cosa from Mount Argentario.

Fig. 8. Hill of Cosa, looking northeast.

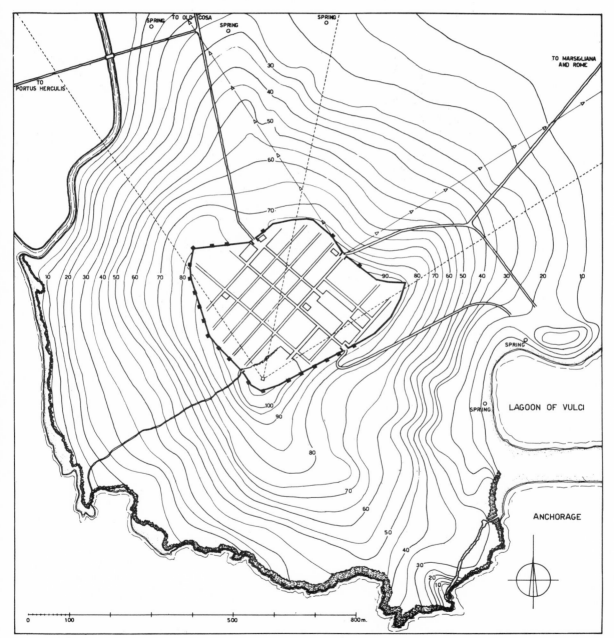

Fig. 9. Hill of Cosa and planned town.

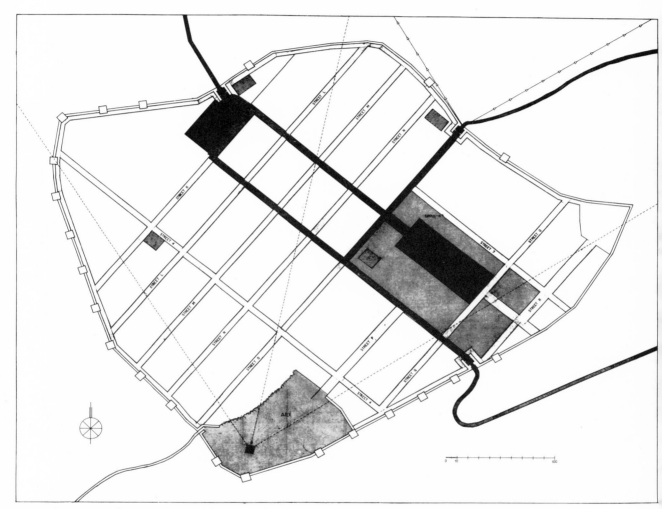

Fig. 10. Town of Cosa, original layout (plan).

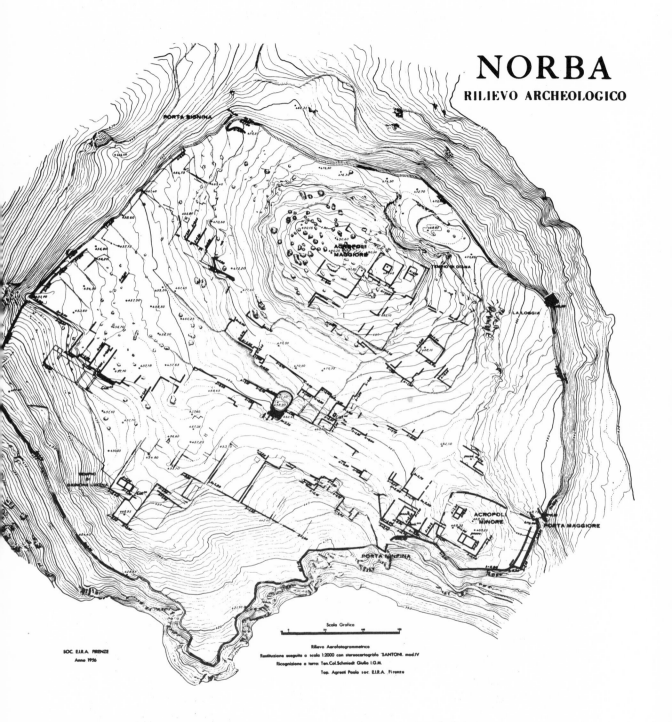

Fig. 11. Norba, actual state (plan).

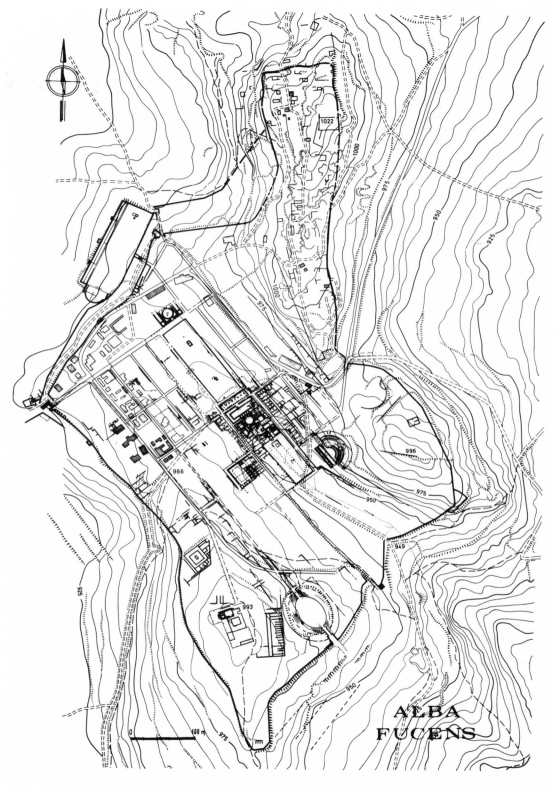

Fig. 12. Alba Fucens, actual state (plan).

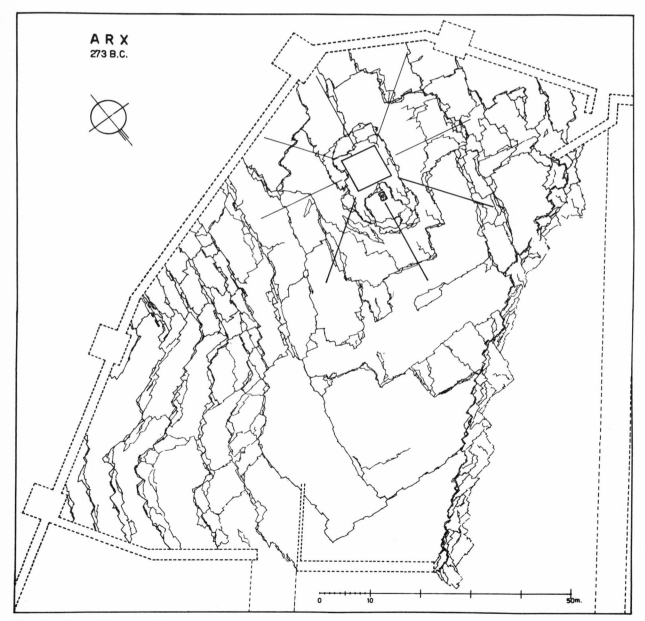

ARX
273 B.C.

Fig. 13. Arx of Cosa in 273 B.C. (plan).

Fig. 16. Wall, southwest front, looking northeast.

Fig. 14. Wall, northeast front, looking northwest.

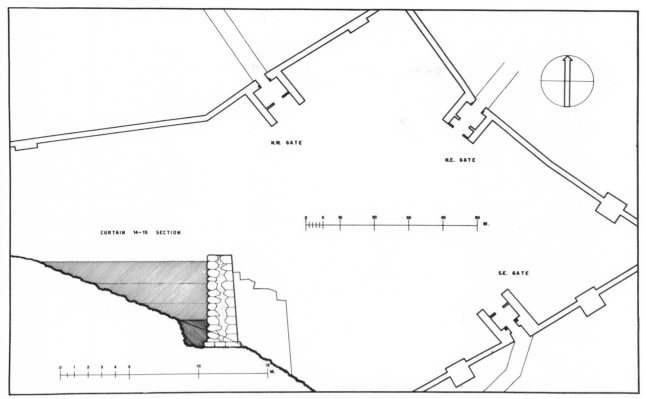

Fig. 15. Gates and towers, section of wall (plan).

Fig. 17. Wall, southeast front, Towers 9 and 10, looking southeast.

Fig. 18. Orbetello (Old Cosa), looking northeast.

Fig. 19. Wall of Orbetello, southwest front.

Fig. 20. Square at northeast gate and storehouse wall.

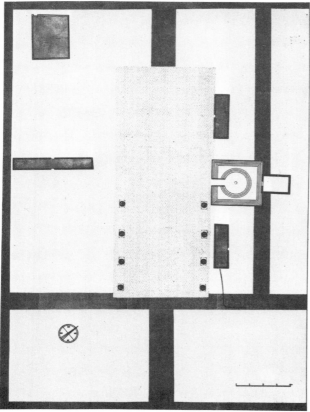

Fig. 21. Forum, first phase, restored (plan).

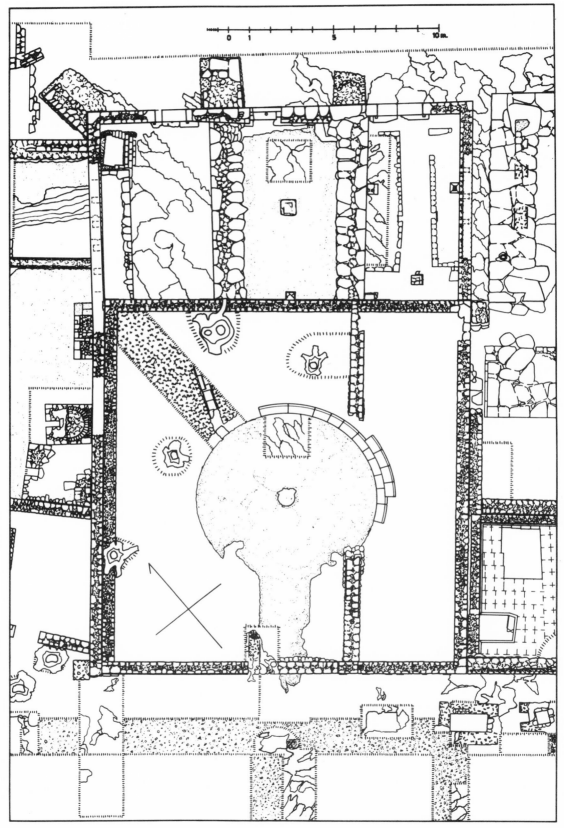

Fig. 22. Comitium and Curia, actual state (plan).

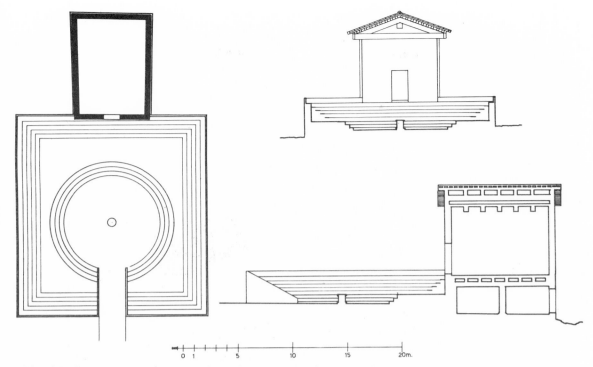

Fig. 23. Comitium and Curia, first phase, restored (plan and sections).

Fig. 24. Forum, northeast side, first phase (elevation, restored).

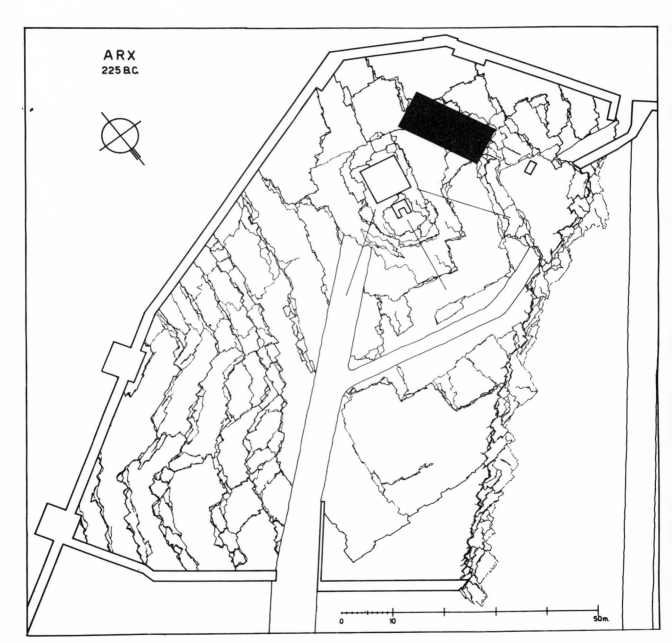

ARX
225 B.C.

0   10   50 m.

Fig. 25. Arx with Temple of Jupiter (plan).

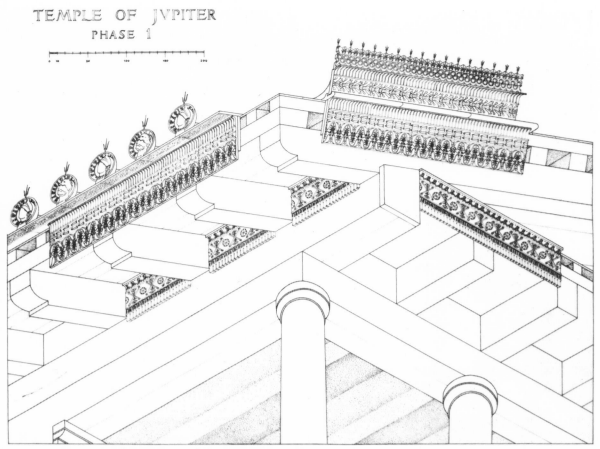

Fig. 26. Temple of Jupiter, roof decoration (isometric).

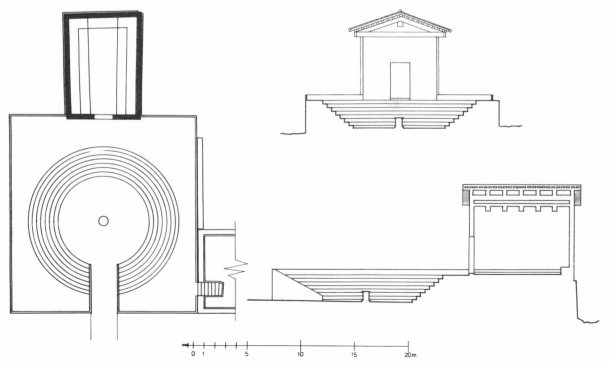

Fig. 27. Comitium and Curia, second phase, restored (plan and sections).

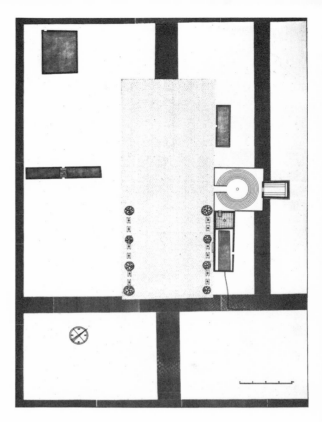

Fig. 29. Forum, second phase, restored (plan).

Fig. 28. Forum, northeast side, planting pits and sockets, looking southeast.

Fig. 30. Forum "Graecostasis," walls, floor, and stair.

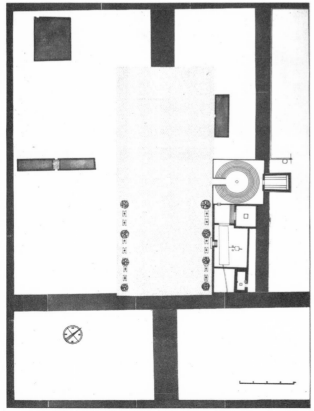

Fig. 31. Forum, third phase, restored (plan).

Fig. 32. Inscription, Concordiae.

Fig. 33. Forum, *carcer,* looking southeast.

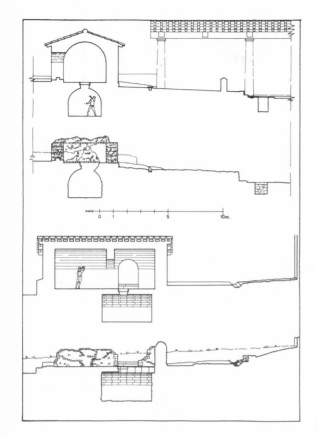

Fig. 34. *Carcer,* actual state
and restored (sections).

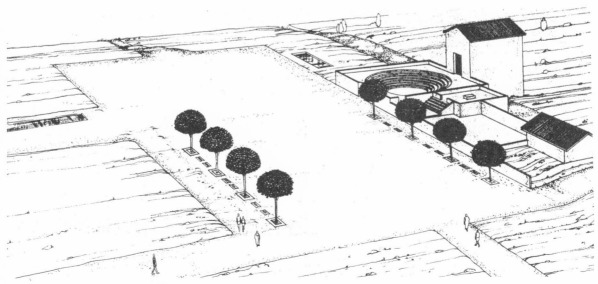

Fig. 35. Forum, third phase, looking north, restored (perspective).

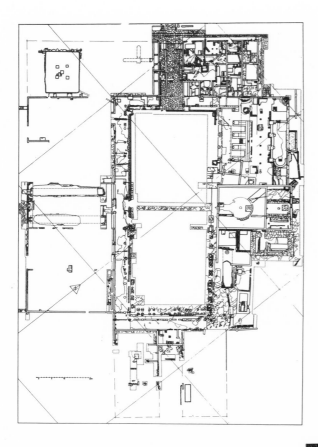

Fig. 36. Forum, actual state (plan).

Fig. 37. Forum, fourth phase, restored (plan).

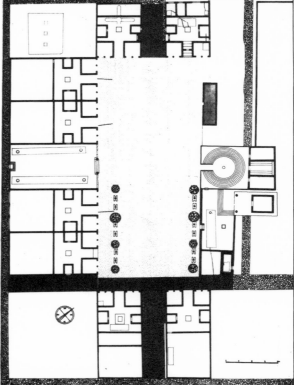

Fig. 38. Forum, Atrium Publicum I and north shops, looking south.
Fig. 39. Atrium Publicum I, restored (sections and elevations).

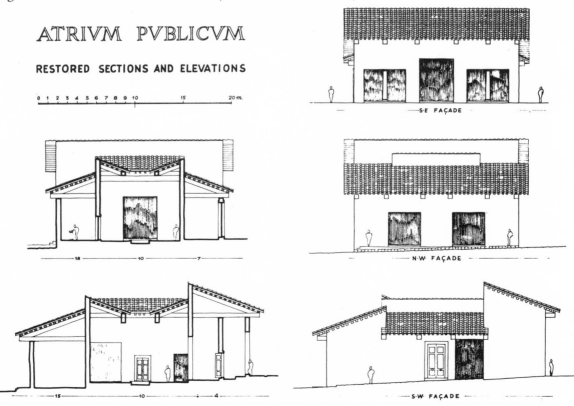

ATRIVM PVBLICVM

RESTORED SECTIONS AND ELEVATIONS

0 1 2 3 4 5 6 7 8 9 10   15   20 m.

S·E FAÇADE

18   10   7

N·W FAÇADE

15   10   4

S·W FAÇADE

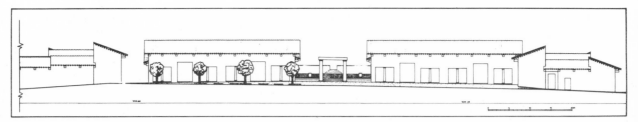

Fig. 40. Forum, southwest side, fourth phase, restored (elevation).

Fig. 41. Temple of Concord (airview).

Fig. 43. Temple of Concord, roof decoration (isometric).

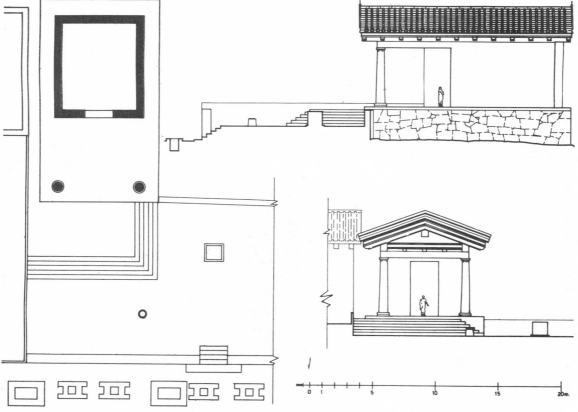

Fig. 42. Temple of Concord, restored (plan and sections).

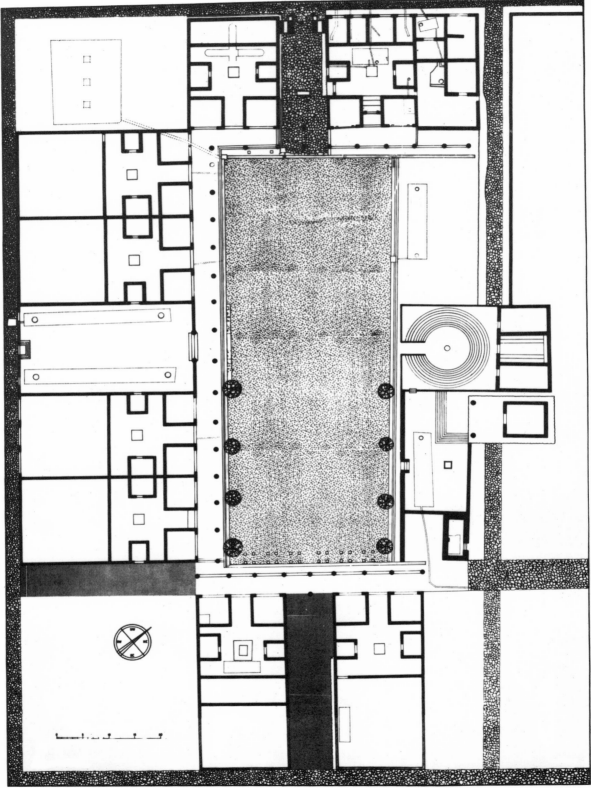

Fig. 44. Forum, fifth phase, restored (plan).

Fig. 45. Forum, northwest portico, looking southwest.

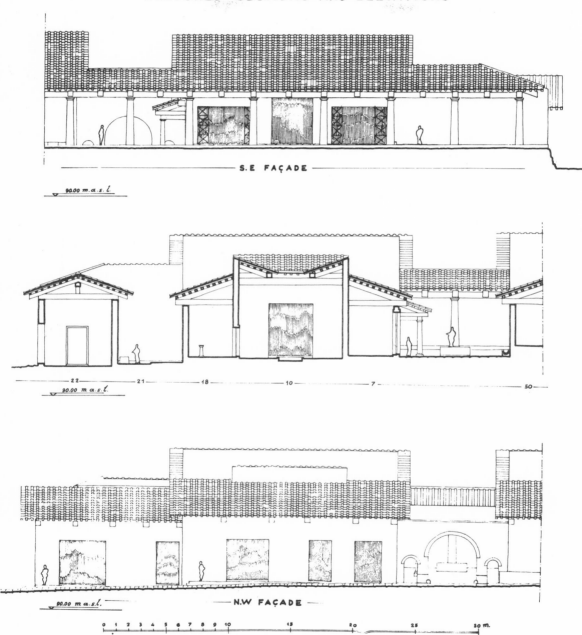

ATRIVM PVBLICVM·TABERNAE·PORTICVS·FORNIX
RESTORED SECTIONS AND ELEVATIONS

S.E FAÇADE

90.00 m.a.s.l.

22   21   18   10   7   50

90.00 m.a.s.l.

90.00 m.a.s.l.

N.W FAÇADE

0 1 2 3 4 5 6 7 8 9 10   15   20   25   30 m.

Fig. 47. Atrium Publicum I, portico, arch, restored (section and elevations).

Fig. 46. Forum, southwest portico, looking southeast.

Fig. 48. Forum, trimmed rock and pavement.

Fig. 49. Forum, step of "bulletin board."

Fig. 50. Street 5, sewer main.

Fig. 51. Forum, Monumental arch, looking southeast.

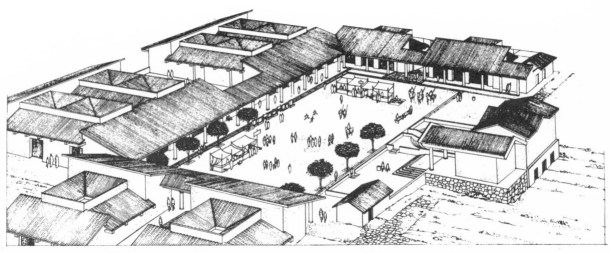

Fig. 52. Forum, fifth phase, looking west, restored (perspective).

Fig. 53. Arx (airview).

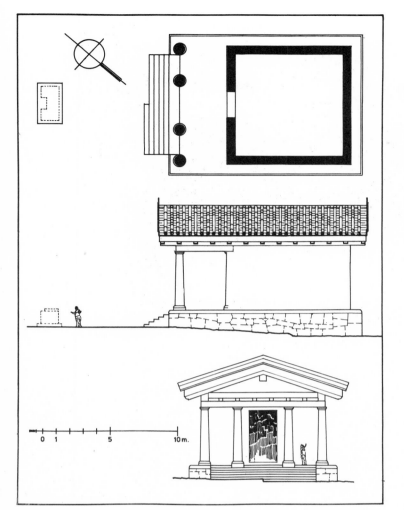

Fig. 54. Temple of Mater Matuta (plan and elevations).

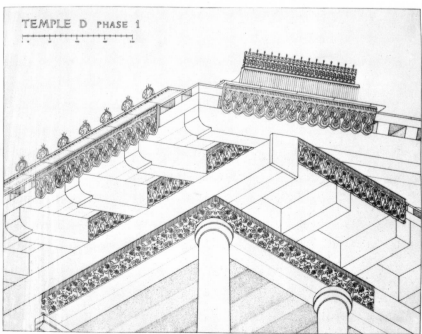

Fig. 55. Temple of Mater Matuta, roof decoration (isometric).

Fig. 56. Temple of Mater Matuta, pedimental sculpture.

Fig. 57. Promontory, dune, and silted lagoon, looking north.

Fig. 58. Scarps and bed
of sluiceway.

Fig. 59. Port of Cosa,
first phase.

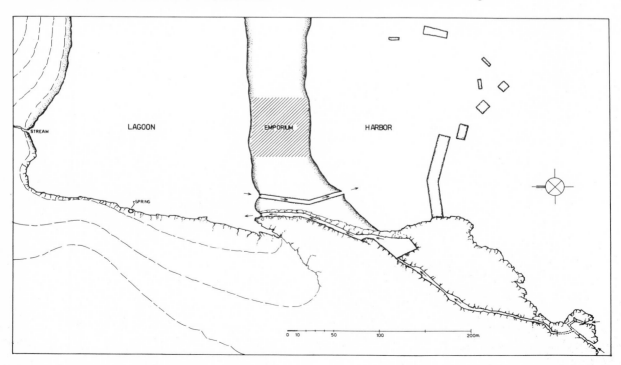

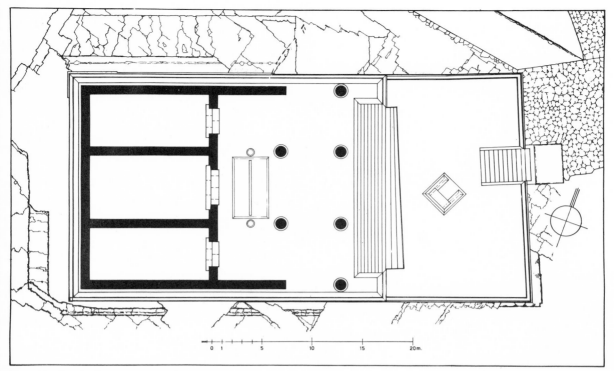

Fig. 60. Capitolium, restored (plan).

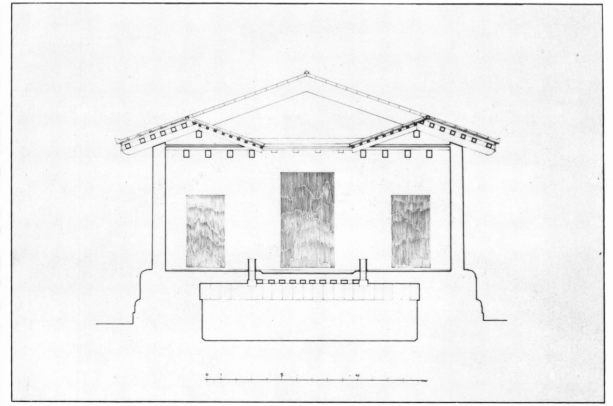

Fig. 63. Capitolium, pronaos and cistern, restored (section).

Fig. 61. Capitolium, podium.

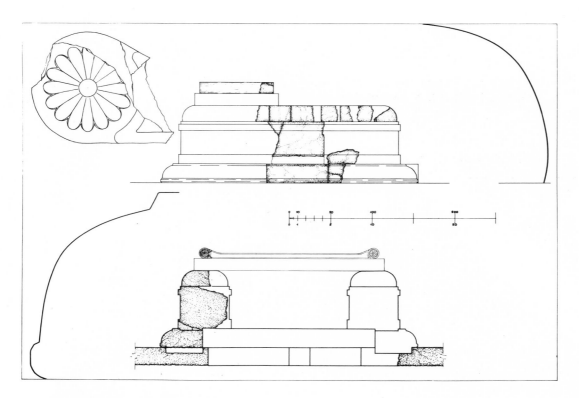

Fig. 64. Capitolium, altar (elevations).

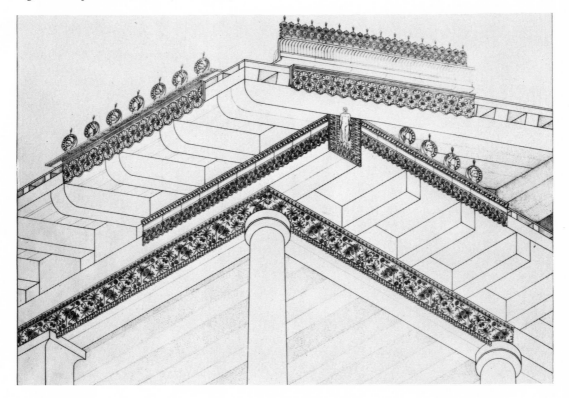

Fig. 66. Capitolium, roof decoration, restored (isometric).

Fig. 62. Capitolium, cistern.

Fig. 65. Capitolium, south flank.

Fig. 67. Ganymede, beam-end sculpture.

Fig. 68. Capitolium and Temple of Mater Matuta, restored (perspective).

Fig. 70. Basilica, restored (plan).

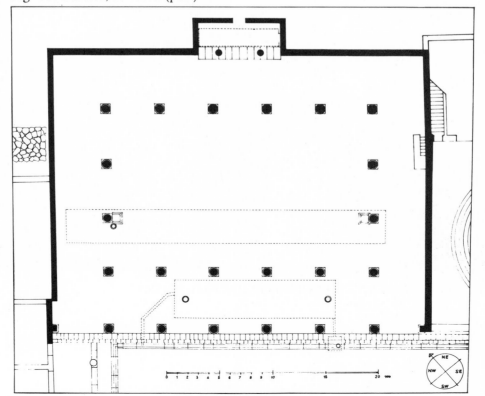

Fig. 69. Atrium Publicum I, basilica, Comitium, and Curia (airview).

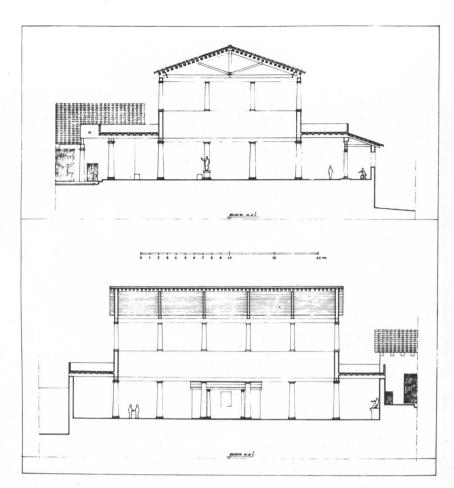

Fig. 71. Basilica, restored (sections).

Fig. 72. Basilica, Ionic capital.

Fig. 74. Ruins of bath building.

Fig. 73. Forum, sixth phase, looking north, restored (perspective).

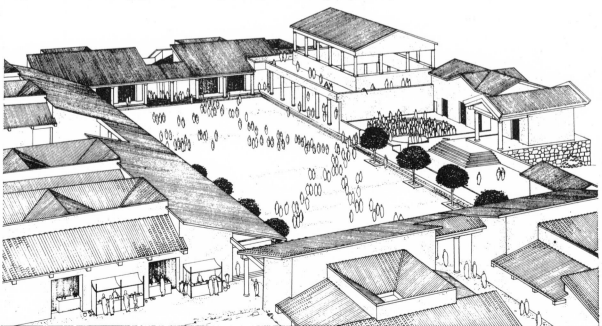

Fig. 75. Port area, looking southwest.

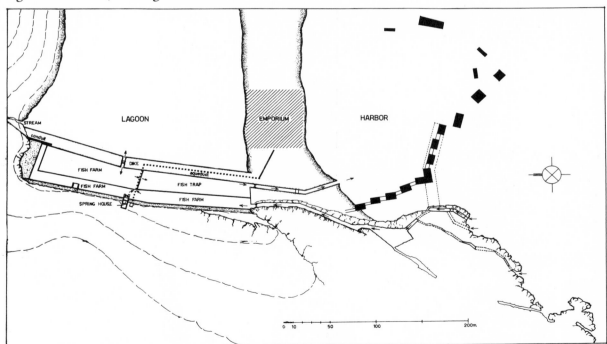

STREAM

conduit

LAGOON

EMPORIUM

HARBOR

DIKE

FISH FARM

aqueduct

FISH FARM   FISH TRAP

SPRING HOUSE   FISH FARM

0 10   50   100   200m.

Fig. 77. Port of Cosa, second phase.

Fig. 76. Outer port (airview).

Fig. 78. Front of springhouse.
Fig. 79. Excavated houses (plan).

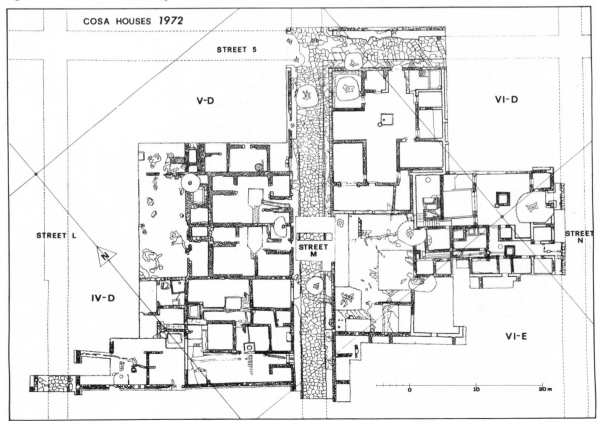

COSA HOUSES 1972

STREET 5

V-D

VI-D

STREET L

STREET M

STREET N

IV-D

VI-E

0   10   20 m

Fig. 80. House, typical cistern.

Fig. 81. Square V-D, earliest houses; Squares V/VI-D/E, houses, first stage (plans).

Fig. 82. V-D houses, looking east.

Fig. 84. Typical waterspout.

Fig. 83. Square V-D, earliest houses (section).

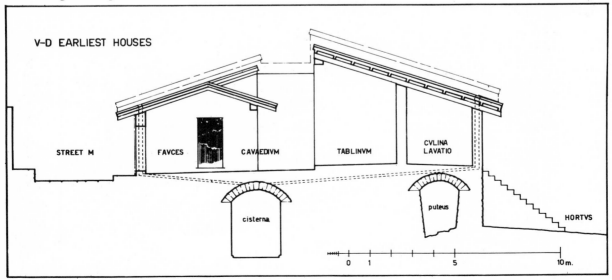

V-D EARLIEST HOUSES

STREET M   FAVCES   CAVAEDIVM   TABLINVM   CVLINA LAVATIO

cisterna   puteus   HORTVS

0   1   5   10 m.

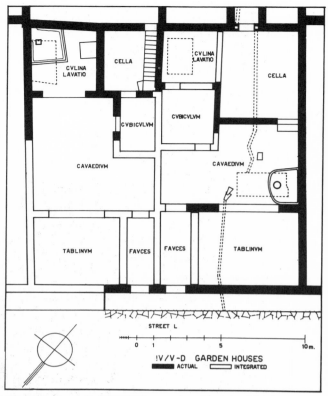

Fig. 85. Squares IV/V-D, garden houses (plan).

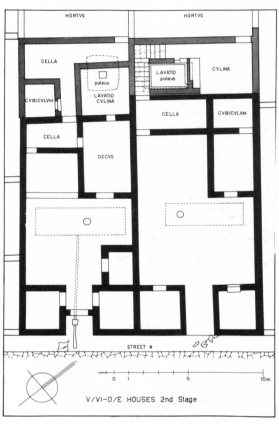

Fig. 86. Squares V/VI-D/E,
extended houses (plan).

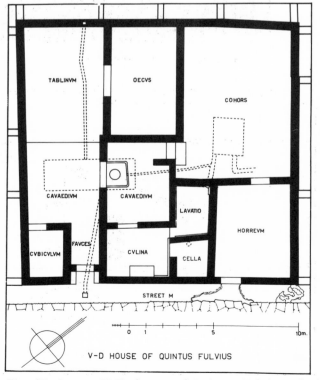

Fig. 87. Square V-D, house of Quintus Fulvius (plan).

Fig. 88. House of Q. Fulvius, coin hoard.

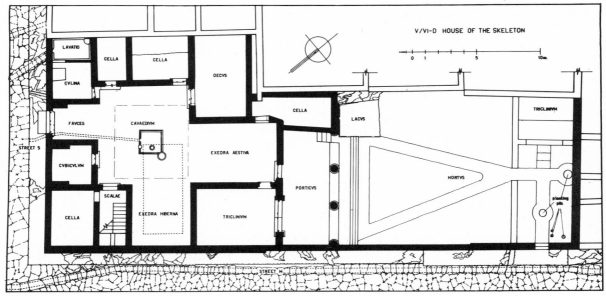

Fig. 89. House of the skeleton (plan).

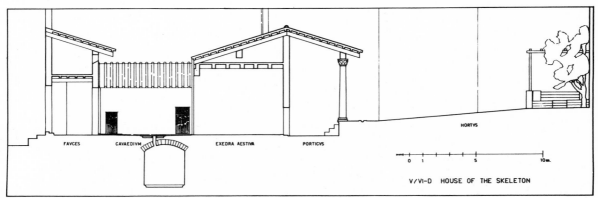

Fig. 90. House of the skeleton (section).

Fig. 91. House of the skeleton, looking southwest.

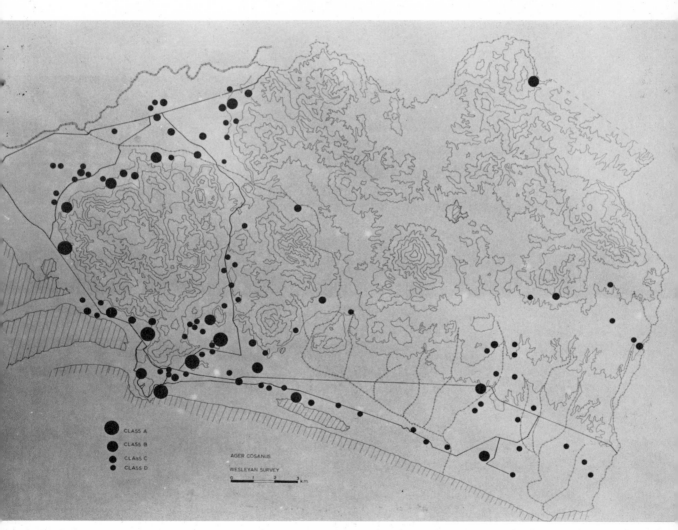

Fig. 92. Ager cosanus, sizes of farm sites.

Fig. 93. Villa of the columns (airview).

Fig. 94. Villa of the seven windows (airview).

Fig. 95. Villa of the seven windows, upper terrace wall.

Fig. 96. Villa of the columns, lower terrace wall.

Fig. 97. Wine pressing room.

Fig. 98. Amphoras of "Sestius" type.

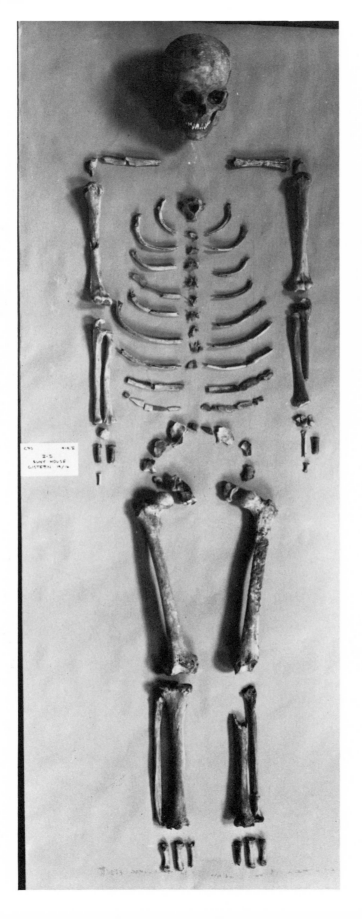

Fig. 99. Skeleton from the cistern of the house of the skeleton.